THE EMPTY NEST

Shelley Bovey is a journalist and broadcaster specialising in women's issues, and a contributor to *The Guardian, Good Housekeeping* and *The Sunday Times*. She is married with three grown-up children, three cats and a dog and lives in Somerset. *The Empty Nest* is her third book.

THE EMPTY NEST

WHEN CHILDREN LEAVE HOME

Shelley Bovey

Pandora
An Imprint of HarperCollins*Publishers*

The author would like to thank the following for kind
permission to quote from published material:
Element Books for *The Wise Woman* by Judy Hall and Dr
Robert Jacobs; HarperCollins*Publishers* for *Breaking the
Bonds* by Dorothy Rowe; Hutchinson Ltd for *To the City*
by Gillian Tindall; The Putnam Publishing Group for *The
Motherline* by Naomi Ruth Lowinsky.

Pandora
An Imprint of HarperCollins*Publishers*
77–85 Fulham Palace Road,
Hammersmith, London W6 8JB
1160 Battery Street,
San Francisco, California 94111–1213

Published by Pandora 1995
1   3   5   7   9   10   8   6   4   2

A catalogue record for this book
is available from the British Library

ISBN 0 04 440898 6

Typeset by
Harper Phototypesetters Limited, Northampton
Printed in Great Britain by
HarperCollinsManufacturing Glasgow

CONTENTS

The only thing worth writing about
is the conflict in the human heart.

William Faulkner

For my children
Jane, Lindsay, Alex,
who taught me to love
and to let go

Preface and
Acknowledgements

From the moment we become pregnant we give hostages to fortune for it is through our children that we are most vulnerable. Carrying and giving birth to a child opens us to the possibility of losing that child; every pregnant woman knows the fear of miscarriage, prematurity, stillbirth or handicap; every mother instinctively checks a sleeping baby to make sure it is still breathing and knows the heart-stopping dread when, for a moment, it appears not to be. As they begin to grow up their health and safety are constantly on our minds, and we look after them and protect them from all possible harm until the time when they claim the right to be autonomous adults and leave home. And then we can no longer keep them safe, or direct the course of their actions. We have to let them go so that they can make lives of their own while we begin a new phase in ours. This is the time when so many women experience feelings of redundancy and loss, commonly known as the *empty nest syndrome*.

When I was asked to write a book about the empty nest syndrome, I recognized the phrase as one used usually in a faintly derogatory way with an implicit suggestion that women are poor creatures whose main purpose in life is over when they reach the conjunction of mid-life, menopause and children leaving home. But 'empty nest' resonated, for me, with wider implications; surely, I thought, it is more than just a matter of giving birth and saying goodbye 20 years later. This time is, I believe, a crucial part of women's lives and their development, a rite of passage largely unrecognized by society, and I wanted to learn how it affected other women. I had found my own children's leaving a devastating experience and I was to discover that this was shared by hundreds of other women from all walks of life, from different backgrounds, cultures and class. As I researched this book, as I spoke to many women, and received letters and written accounts from many more, I learned that this is a time for grieving, for acknowledging loss and working through it. If we allow the process to take place it can also become an exciting time of change, of growth and of opportunity. The passage from our role as active to passive mothers can be a struggle, both within ourselves and some-times with our children as they assert their right to be independent, but I learned that in the end we lose nothing. We do, however, gain a great deal and I am thankful that the sharing of experience with other women and the writing of this book have taught me so much.

I would like to acknowledge and thank all those women, too numerous to name, who have so generously and openly contributed their stories, often with pain and much courage as they strove to articulate and understand their feelings.

I thank Stella Clark, Nancy McBrine Sheehan and Dorothy Stokes for permission to reproduce their poems.

Elizabeth Keogh, of the University of Sussex, did invaluable research into the academic literature of empty nest syndrome. My thanks to her for taking time out from her studies to pursue this work. In the end, we both agreed that what little there was proved too contradictory to draw any conclusions. Surprisingly, this is an area largely ignored by psychologists and sociologists, at least on paper. Fortunately I was able to draw on the wisdom of three people with first hand experience of women at this stage of life; my thanks to Marion Davidson, Tirril Harris of the University of London and Hugh Jenkins of the Institute of Family Therapy.

The writing of this book was interrupted and delayed by a period of illness and I must thank Dr Peter Nixon and Dr Carole Rushford for their care during this time. Dr Nixon's image of 'the servant' saved me from despair when I was in the grip of total writer's block caused by illness.

It has not been an easy book to write and I could not have done it without much encouragement and support. This was forthcoming from several directions and many thanks are due to:

The Group – Tessa Warburg, Janet Laurence, Shirley Toulson and Patricia Pitt. The friends who kept me going – Christina Scott-Moncrieff and Richard Masters, Carol Cox, Gabrielle Palmer, Annette Shaw, Geraldine Kew and Helen Kendall. Thanks too, to Helen for writing some beautiful and original material for inclusion.

And my family. My husband, Alistair stayed calm and cooked supper during the last frantic weeks to deadline. His belief in this book has been immeasurable. My daughters, Jane and Lindsay, gave me much valuable feedback from America and Sussex University respectively, helping me to see the situation from the other side while demonstrating that leaving does not mean losing. Alex, my son, has been indispensable and wonderfully patient. Having dragged me into the nineties by teaching me to use a word processor, he had not bargained for the fact that it would take me the length of the book to learn how to get the hang of it and he has rescued many near disasters. Without him, this book would have been eaten by the computer many times over.

Finally, many thanks to my editor, Belinda Budge, for commitment and support well beyond the call of duty, and to my lovely agent, Serafina Clarke.

PROLOGUE

June 1993

It was hot, swelteringly, sweatingly hot. I stood in the kitchen making lunch for 12. Vegetarian lasagne always goes down well with teenagers. At the kitchen table my friend Gill prepared a huge bowl of salad. We worked in comfortable silence, listening to the constant rise and fall of young voices, feeling the energy that reverberated round the house, smiling at each other at overheard snatches of conversation. My 18-year-old daughter and her friends were getting ready for a five day stay at the annual Glastonbury Festival and excitement was running high.

The sky was that fierce, cloudless blue of midsummer and the sun was blazing. All the doors were open, and brown limbs and brightly coloured clothes flashed past as the gang came and went, loading their hopelessly battered old cars with tents, food and cooking equipment. It seemed that they made the only movement in the landscape; everywhere silent and still with that particular languid heaviness which comes with a very hot day. Their voices broke the silence, carrying clearly round the house and garden and beyond into the surrounding hills.

Lunch round our big table was a babble of excited chatter.

'How many clothes should we take? . . . what if it rains? . . . should we take extra loo paper? Where can I keep my money so it will be safe? I need a mirror, has anyone got a mirror? . . . don't be daft, what do you need a mirror for at a pop festival!'

There were frantic phone calls making last minute arrangements for meeting up with friends.

'Matt can't come till tomorrow. Will you be in Mum so we can leave his ticket with you? What if you're out? Shall I put it in a flowerpot.' Suggestions were offered. 'Not a flowerpot, What if it rains? . . . She can cover it with a stone . . . No, put it . . .'

They were all going to be working at the festival and camping in the same field on the huge site. There were complicated discussions about how much food to take, whose cars to go in, who would share tents and did they have the right number of tickets and entrance passes. After lunch they made a vast pot of tea and took it into the garden where they sat, bare-armed and brown in a circle on the grass. I wanted to capture the scene, somehow preserve it forever.

Suddenly they rose, like a flock of gigantic, brightly coloured birds and took off. They gathered up their bags and equipment, piled it and themselves into impossibly small cars and roared off, waving and calling goodbyes to us through the windows, leaning out as they rounded the corner. And we called back: 'Have a wonderful time.'

Gill and I took our tea to a bench in the shade. The heat was fiery and the sudden silence was heavy, almost oppressive. Some would have called it peaceful but it felt as though the vitality had gone out of the day. We sat in silence for a while then Gill turned to me.

'I do envy you,' she said. 'I hadn't realized how much I missed all this.' Gill's three daughters are in their twenties and all left home several years ago. She thought she had grown accustomed to life without her children, but that day at my house stirred memories which were quite painfully nostalgic.

July 1994

I sit on a bench in the shade of the elder tree, a book in my hand, a cup of tea by my side, listening to the silence. My younger daughter is 19 now and has been at university for a year. She has left home. Her bedroom bears testimony to this fact, its walls bare, plants and clutter and colourful rugs gone. It looks unlived in but then it is. This is how it is when they leave. I have two empty, tidy bedrooms.

My elder daughter is 22 and has been gone for four years now. She has been in America for three of them. From her I have had to learn the foolishness of having preconceived ideas about one's children. The first year in the States was a pre-university year out, working as a nanny. I encouraged her to go. I helped her fill in her application form – she was reticent about displaying her qualities and achievements – but it was her first lesson in selling herself in a competitive world. Not every girl who applied to the American Cultural programme would be accepted and she so much wanted this opportunity.

She finished her A-levels and waited to hear if she had been placed with an American family. In August we went to stay with friends in Cambridge, leaving their number on our answering machine in case the awaited call from America should come through, though it was beginning to seem unlikely. Most students were placed in May or June. One afternoon we went to Ely and I wandered into a gift shop with my younger daughter. On impulse I bought a bear, a silly, soft creature, holding a white handkerchief on which were written in red the words 'I'm going to miss you'. That afternoon in Ely was one of those which stands out in my mind with the unforgettable clarity of certain signifi-cant days. I was filled with something like premonition. When we arrived back at the house the light on the answering machine was blinking and – 'I suppose I'd better check that', said our friend pressing the button. A male voice with a strong American accent rang out into the room, requesting that Jane call him back. As I listened, I knew deep in my gut that this was the beginning of the end of my role as mother to my child.

They wanted her in a week's time. We cut short our stay and went home so she could get ready. I was cheerful, practical, supportive. Inside I felt I was being torn apart. This recent schoolgirl, who such a short time ago had been living out the familiar routine of home at five, tea, homework, supper and bed, interspersed with talking and laughing and family quarrels, chats and outings with friends, was now a woman, ready to leave home, to live in a strange new culture for a whole year. I remember thinking that four seasons would pass until I saw her again and never had time stretched so bleakly before me. It wasn't just the time, though. I was losing my child. She would come back, but she would be someone else, changed and shaped by people and influences which had nothing to do with me. I would never see the child Jane again.

And so it was. At first, I counted weeks – then as the year turned, I began to relax. Only a few months, a few weeks – and in September the following year she was home. There was no sign of the schoolgirl, she had travelled far beyond that and acquired a sophistication that was unfamiliar. She went to university and I found this an 'acceptable' way to leave home. I learned later that we cannot prejudge what our children should do on the basis of what feels comfortable for us. It never works. It catches us out because it shows that we are not open to whatever our children, independent, separate beings that they are, may decide to do.

At the end of her first university year, Jane told us that she was returning to America. She had missed the family badly, she preferred the life over there and she wanted to see if she could get into college. Two years later, she is happy and settled, enjoying her course at college and is fulfilled at being back with the family. Although we keep in touch regularly I do not know when, or if she will ever come back to us but I do know that I have no choice or influence in the matter.

I thought it would be much easier when my second daughter left for university. There would be no long separations, after all, and we could keep in touch by phone. She would be home for holidays. I imagined this meaning a return to what it was like before – the house full of young people, me making huge meals for hungry bodies, rows of them asleep on the sitting room floor after a night out. In the Christmas holidays it was very much like that and the house felt normal again. But university means the formation of new groups of friends and though Lindsay's friends from home will be life-long, they too are forging off in new directions, basing themselves in new places. This is the place of familiarity where they grew up. Now they need to explore beyond its comfortable confines.

And that is why this summer I sit in a silent garden. When I get into my car, I do not jump out of my skin as Radio One blasts forth as soon as I turn the ignition on. The dial remains set

sedately on Radio Four. And once again I find myself caught out
by preconceived notions. I had looked forward to the summer
holidays but the close-knit group which formed during that first
year at Sussex University have strong bonds that make them want
to spend the summer together. And so they have remained in
Brighton, sharing houses, working in burger bars and pizza places
and shops, running down to the beach at every opportunity,
cooking, drinking, laughing and enjoying themselves. And I
know it is right that it should be this way.

But I have not yet had to face the final phase. My son is 16 and
still at home. Quieter, more solitary than Lindsay, he does not – as
yet, anyway – lead the hectic, people-filled life that she did when
she lived at home. The dynamics of the family have changed radically. He is now an only child, with the loneliness that goes with
it, and I know that I have to be careful not to cling to him, my
last one. In two years, he too will leave and the phases of my
nest emptying will be complete.

If the sadness and loss I feel at the girls' departures is a measure
of what is to come, I know that I have to begin to prepare for the
final leaving now and not wait until it is upon me.

A breeze has got up and it is cold now in the shade. As I close
my book and rise from the bench, I hear the familiar click of the
gate. It carries with it a warm feeling of anticipation. My son is
returning from his walk with the dog and we will go indoors, chat
for a few minutes, make a drink, probably argue good-naturedly
about something before he goes to his room and I go back to the
word-processor.

But it will not always be like this. Before long my nest will be
truly empty. I think of the pain and the sense of bereavement
expressed by so many of the women who have written and spoken
to me about their experiences of their children leaving. This book
is about letting go, moving forward, embracing the next phase of
life. But first the pain and the grief must be acknowledged, given
room, listened to. That is also what this book is about and I will
not know until I have written it how we move from one state to
the other. With the help of the hundreds of women who have
shared with me their losses I hope to find out.

1 MEMORIES, DREAMS, REFLECTIONS

The child, in the decisive first years of his life, has the experience of his mother as an all-enveloping, protective, nourishing power. Mother is food; she is love; she is warmth; she is earth. To be loved by her means to be alive, to be rooted, to be at home. *Erich Fromm*

When I had my first child I suddenly realized that this was a completely different kind of love from any other. For the very first time I realized that here was someone I would die for or kill for and I'd never ever felt like that about anybody before. *Alice Thomas Ellis*

When a baby is born, we talk about bonding with it and yet, in a strangely paradoxical way those bonds begin to loosen as soon as it leaves the womb and becomes a separate person. It is not a coincidence that people who remain unhealthily attached to their parents in adulthood are sometimes referred to as not having cut the umbilical cord. It is from that moment that our children begin to assert their independence; to take the first steps towards leaving us.

It never occurs to us at that stage, but it is easy to witness, in a litter of kittens for instance. Blind and helpless at birth, spending their days fastened onto the source of nourishment, yet in six short weeks they are fully independent. In between those two points, they can be seen exploring the outside world, tentatively at first, then more boldly and gradually rejecting their mother's restraining presence until finally they do not even bother to return to the box or bed where they grew up but find a place of their own.

When a baby grabs the spoon from us and tries messily to feed herself, when she takes those first triumphant steps or insists on dressing herself long before she is really able to do so, she is beginning the move towards autonomy and individuality. This can be seen so clearly in the two-year-old's tantrums which are saying in the strongest possible terms 'I am me and I want to do this my way'. There are enormous similarities between these tantrums and the rebellious moods and slammed doors of teenagers. With the latter we might have some understanding of their need to assert themselves as separate from us but the two-year-old is no less passionate in demonstrating that same need.

We do not recognize it at that age, though. We do not see the leap our child has made from helpless baby to independent, wilful child or appreciate that this is part of the journey away from us. The wise parent allows the small child to struggle with its clothes while standing by patiently when it would be so much quicker to do it for him. 'Let I do it' is a cry which rings out in some form in every house where there is a small child and it is a forerunner of the grown child's bid for final independence and separateness.

In her book *Of Woman Born*, Adrienne Rich recognizes this dichotomy as not only the child's need for separateness, but the mother's too. The baby, she says, gains its first sense of its own existence from its mother's response, as though in the mother's touch, gestures and expression, the child receives the message 'You are there'. And the mother, too, she says is:

> discovering her own existence newly. She is connected with this other being by the most mundane and the most invisible strands, in a way she can be connected with no one else except in the deep past of her infant connection with her own mother. And she, too, needs to struggle from that one-to-one intensity into new realization, or reaffirmation of her being-unto-herself.

Rich likens this intensity of union to the sexual act and just as lovers have to part after sex and become separate individuals again 'so the mother has to wean herself from the infant and the infant from herself'.

In some of the accounts I received from women about their feelings about children leaving, I noticed an awareness of this early separation. Hilary wrote:

> After all, practically from the day they're born, we are not only preparing children for their adult life, more importantly we are practising letting go ourselves. Their first steps, their first bike, the day you leave them screaming (them, not you!) at Playgroup; as they change from being Mummy's little helpers, who'll come shopping without a murmur, into those other beings who wouldn't be seen dead with their mum and who certainly won't let you into the bathroom to wash their hair. Through the teenage years of staying out late, or staying out all night – all these are trials sent to desensitize mothers in readiness for the day when they're gone altogether.

Separateness is not the same as separation but it can feel that way. Probably the first time we experience this is when our child starts playschool. I am reminded of the poignant television commercial in which a mother leaves her small boy at a playgroup, both of them looking tremulous and uncertain. Sitting in a group of strangers, the little boy reaches for his jacket, buries his nose in it and is reassured by the familiar smell of fabric softener – a link with home. Sentimental maybe, but it illustrates what is often a difficult transition for mother and child – the first episode of leaving home. The following are some women's reactions to this milestone:

> Paula
> I remember leaving my daughter at the village hall Playgroup – it suddenly seemed the most enormous place and she looked so small. As I turned to go, she started crying and was picked up by one of the helpers. I wanted to rush over and take her home with me – but I realized I had to let her go and find her feet.

Jane

My son started nursery school just before his third birthday. I had prepared him well and he was happy and confident. On the first day, he was shown to a miniature desk and given some books and coloured pencils. He didn't even glance in my direction! I was so glad he settled in so well but it was incredibly lonely going home to an empty house. It was then I decided to have another baby.

Camilla

I went back to work shortly after Clare was born so the nanny took her to nursery school. I didn't feel any different – I spent time with her as always when I came home from work. As far as I was concerned it was a normal part of her growing up. I have to admit, though, now she is grown up that I look back and wish I had some memories of those first stages in her life – but the reality is I chose to continue my career and I'm not sure I would do things any differently if I had my time again.

Judy

My son didn't want to go to playschool. At first I tried to persuade, bribe, get angry with him but then I thought, Why do this to him before I have to? He was happy at home, there's no law that says they have to go to playschool and at five he would be going to school anyway. Was I over-protective? To be honest, I think it was as much for my sake as his – I liked having him at home and I dreaded losing that close bond.

Perhaps not surprisingly, I found a correlation between these accounts of the first leaving with the final departure from home – not from the children's point of view, but that of the mothers. Paula felt immense sadness when her children finally left home, but still had the same conviction that she must let them go and find their own feet. Jane says rather ruefully that her son, an only child (the second baby never appeared) left home with the same 'never a backward glance' attitude with which he had started nursery school, but feels that this reflects successful parenting on her part. Camilla enjoys an excellent relationship with her two daughters but says she was 'far too busy to get in a state about them leaving home'. Judy, who has suffered a great deal of depression since her sons finally left a year ago feels defensive about the fact that she wishes they could have stayed, 'at least in the neighbourhood. I loved them being at home'.

If playgroup or nursery school is the first tentative step towards the time when our children leave us finally, school is a veritable leap. When I spoke to the mothers of grown-up children about the first day at school, they all had vivid memories:

The parents weren't allowed into the school playground – we all waited at the gates to watch them. He was crying his eyes out and no one took any notice. Then the bell went and they had to form lines outside their classroom door. I had a last glimpse of this little tear-stained face and I felt like a monster. I went home and howled. I found out later that he settled down almost as soon as he was inside but it took me weeks, I can tell you.

She begged not to go and when it came to it, she clung on so hard, I could hardly disentangle her from my skirt. Her infant teacher came and took her hand but she clung even harder. So this lovely, motherly teacher picked her up and cuddled her then took her inside. This ritual went on for weeks and it tore me apart every time. I think sending her to school was the hardest thing I ever did.

I was so proud of her when she started school. She went off that first day with her little red and blue uniform and brand new sandals that were too big for her, with her hair in little plaits with ribbons on. I couldn't wait for three o'clock when I could fetch her and she was so excited about it all. I remember going home and getting her a drink and biscuit while she told me all about it and that little ritual took place with all of them until the last one left school at eighteen.

I took a day off work to take the twins to school for the first time. It was a day I shall never forget and though I wasn't at home when they got back every day, that first day memory is very precious. It's a rite of passage and I was glad I was there to witness it.

This time, I found an even stronger link between women's feelings about their children starting school and their leaving home. Every woman I spoke to about beginning school had strong emotions when recalling those memories but the emotions varied a great deal. For some, the loosening of that particular bond was extremely painful; they felt a sadness that was magnified when the final parting came. For others the emotions were nostalgic, perhaps, but they did not recall a particular sense of loss.

I do not feel that there is any place here for judgment of any kind. It would be futile and useless to say that the women who suffered at this stage were too clingy, too protective – the fact is that they had more emotional investment in their children at this stage than did the women who found the letting go easier. Nor is the evidence conclusive that women who find it hard to see their small children start to go out into the world are likely to cling when it is time for them to leave home. I feel it is important to make this point because criticism is so often levelled at mothers who are perceived to be over-involved with their children. In many cases they may be but there are good reasons for this. Ideally, we should begin preparing for our children's independence from the moment they are born. We should encourage their separateness, rejoice at each step they take to establish themselves as individuals in their own right. Most women do this but we don't always get it right. We should be leading our own separate lives, too, apart from our children, even at this stage so that our identities are not just as mothers, for it is in the very nature of motherhood that we will get it wrong a good deal of the time.

'A mother's place is in the wrong,' Katherine Whitehorn once said. I feel that women who find it difficult and painful to see their children go, at whatever stage, should be supported and not blamed. Letters I received showed how powerful the memories of this time of early childhood are, and how they are revived when the children leave. The empty nest is a time to look forward but for many, it is necessary to look back first, to grieve for the lost times before it is possible to move on.

It should not be underestimated that for many women their child starting school foreshadows that final parting, creating something deep and visceral, like a precognition of how it will be when they finally leave. Handing over small children to the care of others prefigures the independence that grown children claim for themselves; both are times when the child begins to develop thoughts and ideas that come not from the home or from their parents but from other people, other influences. And both situations can set up feelings of emptiness and redundancy.

Sarah, preparing now for her last child to leave, wrote and told me how she felt when he went to school:

I feel ashamed to tell you this – I've never told anyone else. I had been a little sad when my daughter, who is the elder child, started school, but it was the kind of sadness that I think most mothers experience. Then it was William's turn. He was due to start after the Easter holidays, just before his fifth birthday. A few weeks before the start of term I started waking in the night in floods of tears. I couldn't bear the thought of losing him – I know how ridiculous this sounds but I felt as though I were being bereaved. I couldn't tell anybody, not even my husband. I knew I would be considered mad, or a terrible, clinging monster of a mother. Every day I talked to myself, told myself to buck up, that kind of thing. I prepared William well for school and he was quite happy about the idea. I never showed him how I felt, obviously. But no amount of telling myself not to be so stupid could affect what happened in my sleep and it was then that it all came out. I actually woke myself up with my sobbing. It's hard to explain exactly what I felt I was losing – perhaps the two years we'd had together since my daughter had gone to school but it was deeper than that. I felt he would no longer be mine – and I know that's a terrible, possessive thing to say but I'm trying to be honest.

In the event, the reality was nothing like as bad as the anticipation. I hated the first day at school but after a week or so it was alright. I never experienced the loss I felt before he went so I suppose it was some kind of fear, probably related to losses I experienced in my own childhood. I found that my relationship with William was different but no less precious. He would come home from school and tell me what he'd done and I have to say that I did appreciate having some time to myself. Now that it's nearly time for him to leave home, I'm experiencing the same dread, though this time it's conscious, not in my sleep. It's the same feeling of impending bereavement but I'm hoping that it will be like the school time – that the reality won't be as bad as what I'm going through now. I feel fairly confident that our relationship will be as close as ever, though, like the time he went to school, it will change because this is another stage in his life. He has to go through it – and so do I.

Sarah was not the only woman to find that her reactions and feelings about a child leaving home had their echoes all those years ago when that same child started school. One woman came across a poem she wrote just before her son went to school:

It really startled and amazed me. The feelings in it are exactly the same ones I'm experiencing now as I wait for my son to start university in the autumn. What is so uncanny is that it could have been written now about this situation but it was written 15 years ago about another entirely different one. The only difference is that this time I know he can see to his own needs! I'd forgotten I still had it – I'd forgotten I'd even written it.

She gave me a copy of the poem:

The Parting
A Mother's feelings when her child starts school.

It is here and must be faced.
Threads close-woven on a loom now separate
And go their different ways;
This has to be in order to create
The pattern of the tapestry.

> The parallel of years must change;
> Ahead divergence – a path which now will fork.
> A painful wrench of symbiotic union.
> Will he cleave to others as he has to me?
> And will they know and understand his needs?
> And when they tell me of the freedom that I'll gain
> They cannot know the pain of tearing loss,
> The isolation, phantom agony of amputated limb.
> For who would understand that I would rather be
> Captive still, in that precious captivity?

Agony aunt and journalist Virginia Ironside echoed this when she wrote about her son Will who had just left home to travel to India:

> Nineteen years ago, when he had just been born and lay in a carrycot beside me, I remember feeling that it was not a baby under the little blanket, but one of my own limbs. The day he left for India, the feelings were the same. (*The Times*, 6.4.93.)

And magazine editor, Janice Bhend, who wrote to me:

> I've often thought that having your children grow up on you is akin to bereavement. When they were little and I left them for a day or so, I used to feel I needed a label around my neck saying 'I have two sons at home, you know,' they were so very much a part of me that when I was away from them it was like having an arm or a leg missing. These day I look unbelievingly at those photos on the piano of the dear little boys in matinée jackets and later in school uniforms and wonder 'where did they go, what became of them?' and realize they are gone for ever.

It is not surprising when our children leave to begin their own adult lives that we should relive the memories of their childhoods. No free-thinking feminist, advocating that a mother of grown children should live her own life, can deny or diminish the impact on a woman of 20-odd years of child-rearing. It is woven into our minds, our bodies, our thoughts and our souls and when it changes, like all changes, it is alarming. It is human nature that when anything comes to an end, we look back and reflect on it with nostalgia. This is not only natural, it is necessary – to gather together memories, to reflect on them before we can be ready to leave them as memories. There is bound to be a longing for the past we can no longer experience. As Virginia Ironside put it:

> What if what you enjoy more than anything in the world is looking after little people and raising them up to be big people? What if, like me, you would prefer by far to make a suit out of black cardboard, wire and old sheets for your son to wear in the Ants' Chorus at primary school than take an Open University course? . . . What if you would much prefer to be watching your child hurtle down the Log Flume at Thorpe Park or winning the three-legged race at school . . . or sitting on the sofa, with an arm round a warm, giggling body watching the Batman re-runs on Channel Four? (*The Independent*, 14.9.93)

And that is part of the anguish. We have lost those things and cannot choose to have them again. We can divest these longings of their power to hurt us by allowing ourselves to experience them, to go through the pain of regret until they lose their immediacy, their potency and fade a little, making room for new sets of impressions, different kinds of enjoyment. The worst thing we can do is to deny the existence of these immensely powerful feelings, to shut them up in a box in our mind where they will do harm by being suppressed.

When our children leave us, we and they are saying farewell to their childhood and I think it is useful for both parent and child to acknowledge this, preferably together. Looking through photographs, rummaging through accumulated possessions, whether toys, drawings, school books or raffia mats lovingly and clumsily made at primary school is a good way of going back to the past, exclaiming, remembering, laughing. When my daughters left, I had a pine chest containing all their drawings and school books from the very beginning. We went through them with much laughter and exclamations of 'I remember that – I did that in Mrs Smith's class.' For us all, it was a delightful evocation of their childhood and when we closed the lid of the chest I decided that when they had gone, it would be time to have a clear out. Did I really need to keep Junior Maths Book 1? Of course I didn't and I did a great pruning job. But I kept their early drawings and little letters and news books from school – the ones teachers get them to write so that they find out all our secrets; 'Daddy couldn't go to work today becos Mummy had woshed all his trouwsers and she diden't dry them.'

One friend said she didn't miss those childhood days because she could call them back any time she wanted by getting out the reminders – those early drawings, photographs and little clothes. And then she puts them away again and returns herself to the present.

When my elder daughter had left to go to America, I felt rather like my cat who carried socks around when her kittens started going! I trawled endlessly through boxes of photographs, taking out the best ones of their childhood and putting them in frames. Soon I had a pretty big collection which produced a pleasant spin-off; friends and family started giving me photo frames for birthdays and Christmas. The result is that I now have some really beautiful and unusual frames and a collection of photos which includes my whole, extended family with my children from birth to the present day. It is a visual record of their growing up and of the relatives who played such important parts in their lives.

Many women who have written and spoken to me about this time have found that it is the few months *before* the final parting which are full of anxiety and apprehension. Time is suspended – they have not gone but nor are they fully here and both mother and child wonder what it will be like and how they will cope – the mother, with the separation and her new life, and the child with what lies ahead in the new and adult future. It is at this time that the bridge between their childhood and their adult selves is shaky. When they are children, we don't project forward and imagine them as adults, but when we realize that they have arrived at this place, it is not uncommon to look back with a sense of panic.

It is important to acknowledge whatever pain or anxiety comes up for us at this time. Like any other feeling, if it is suppressed, it will surface somehow, often in a more distressing way than if we had allowed it in the first place. I remember thinking that I must be strong and positive when I knew my first child would be leaving to live abroad. I admitted no weakness to myself – I knew I had to let go and I was determined I would do it well. I did not listen to the other part of me that needed to mourn for the passing of childhood and so it came to me in my sleep and I began to have a recurrent dream:

> It is Christmas Eve. I am in the kitchen of the cottage where we lived when the children were small and I am making mince pies as I always have on the afternoon of Christmas Eve. The children are playing on the floor and there is a feeling of perfect contentment. I can feel the warmth of the kitchen round me. I am listening to the service of nine lessons and carols from Kings College, Cambridge. I start to wake up and I realize that I am dreaming. For a time I cling onto the dream, not wanting to leave it. I can hear with absolute clarity the carol being sung – *In the Bleak Midwinter* – the purity of the solo voice, the warmth of the kitchen and the children playing are all more real than the bed in which I know I am waking, but the return to reality is inexorable and both the sound of the carol and the Christmas Eve scene of long ago fade. I try to hold it but it dissolves. I wake, weeping.

I have not had that dream for four years but I can recall the intensity of the grief that accompanied it as vividly as if it were yesterday. The scene it contains represents the happiest times of those years. Christmas and childhood together are symbols of a wellbeing and joy which may be more metaphorical than actual but certainly provides a powerful symbol in a dream.

The childhood home also influences the way we may feel at this time. Many people decide to move house around the time their children leave home, as we did. I felt it was a positive step, a new beginning but I did not take account of what I was leaving behind until the day we moved. My diary records how I stayed behind long after the removal men and the family had departed. I went from room to room, remembering, and in each room I could hear the voices of the children at different ages, as though in layers and I saw the events of the years like a kaleidoscope. I recalled countless children's parties and games in the garden. I saw their bedrooms as they went through the changes from pink walls to black and white posters for the girls and trains puffing through an endless, pastoral picture book wallpaper to bright primary colours for my son. I remembered tears at bedtime, the laughter and squabbles and all the pets they had, bedtime stories and looking in at small shapes under bedclothes when we went to bed.

Clearing out my study recently, I found a letter to my daughter in America, which I had obviously never intended to send:

> . . . It's been a difficult year. The familiarity and rhythm of our lives has gone – you going to school, coming home at the same time every day, all of us round the kitchen table for supper, catching up with each other, a landmark in the day, something solid and reliable. Family outings and holidays – and then upheaval. What I didn't realize at the time was that I was losing you and my home at the same time. All my memories, all your childhood were contained in that house. Memories somehow become part of the fabric of a place, they are imprinted in the walls. The chimney in my study was always Father Christmas' chimney – that same room used to be your bedroom and then Lindsay's.
>
> I remember you lying in bed there with that terrible illness you had. You got thinner and thinner till it seemed all we could see of you was these great big eyes and we called it your stick insect disease . . .

I can see now that it was too much all at once. If you are facing the empty nest, which is a major life change, whichever way you feel about it, I would suggest that you put off a house move for a year or so, in the same way that it is unwise for a bereaved person to make such a radical change immediately after a loss. In both cases, you need time to assimilate the change in the place which holds the memories before being able to move on, literally and emotionally.

Now that my children are grown I feel I have integrated their childhoods with the adults they have become. I may have empty rooms, but the house is full of pictures which link the past to the present. Three little pairs of first-size red Wellingtons stand amid the clutter of a grown-up family – the children love them and laugh at the notion they were ever that small.

What is important is now and although memories are an essential part of our lives, the tragedy comes when people cannot see the present because their perception is obscured, either by longing for the past or worrying about the future. Mourning the past for a while is natural but we have to transform that mourning into a willingness to go forward.

One woman said to me: 'I can't help thinking of Robert Browning's poem about England – I want to *recapture that first, fine careless rapture* that was my children's childhood. I feel that same kind of aching for something far away. I want to be able to turn the clock back.'

In the letter to my elder daughter, which was never sent, I wrote:

Only a year ago, Lindsay was still at school and played her clarinet all the time. Now that she's left she never touches it. The silent clarinet seems to me to be symbolic of all the changes. I am trying to catch up with the reality of this change and know I must let go, not only of you three, but of the past. Sometimes I feel an overwhelming longing to be back in our old kitchen with you all around me, but I know in my head that if one can let go of the past, turn away and have the courage to look in a new direction, there are even richer rewards.

There is often a chasm between knowing something intellectually and feeling it in the heart. Though for some the experience is simultaneous, the transition between the two is not always easy, and for many women facing the empty nest, the bridge across the abyss can seem a very rickety one indeed. It takes courage, guidance and support to cross it.

Sometimes I hear childish voices calling, I hear the wind and the sea and the cry of seagulls and I am back in Cornwall where we spent our holidays when they were small. I can see three little figures making sandcastles on the beach, or running into the sea, two with plaits, one with a mass of red curls – then the image grows fainter and superimposed on it I see clearer, stronger pictures of my children as they are now, grown-up, beautiful, independent and planning their futures – and I realize that every stage of their lives is precious, none less or more so than any other.

2 WHAT IS EMPTY NEST SYNDROME?

Empty – containing nothing, without inhabitants, vacant or unoccupied; carrying no load, passengers, etc.; without purpose, substance or value; not expressive or vital; vacant.

Nest – a number of animals of the same species and their young occupying a common habitat; a cosy or secluded place. *Collins English Dictionary*

> Your children are not your children.
> They are the sons and daughters of Life's longing for
>   itself.
> They come through you but not from you,
> And though they are with you they belong not to
>   you. *'The Prophet', Kahlil Gibran*

It's a familiar enough phrase – empty nest syndrome – but what does it really mean? Literally, it signals the time when the job of active mothering is finished, when our children leave home and we are no longer responsible for them, although it is in the nature of parents to worry about their children, whatever age they are. But why is it a syndrome, – a sociologically and psychologically recognized condition? What does the empty nest mean? And how does it change our lives? What happens to the woman who for 20 years or more has been *mother* and who does she become?

Among the large number of women who have talked or written to me for this book, I found that the empty nest experience fell roughly into two categories. Some mothers suffer a sense of loss and bereavement, often accompanied by depression, loss of purpose and identity; while others feel it is a time of opportunity, the opening of a new phase in their lives. The majority of the women who contacted me came into the former category, but with time have moved on into the latter. Psychologists, on the whole, recognize that it is a time of mourning and enormous adjustment, but not all agree on that, and some sociologists actually deny the existence of empty nest syndrome.

I feel at this point that I should establish that I do not propose in this book to enter into an academic debate. I have read much of the research on women at mid-life and find it confusing and contradictory. Some studies suggest that mid-life women suffer a greater incidence of depression, due to the loss of the 'female role'. Other studies claim that depression is significantly less likely to occur at this stage. Some research reports the likelihood of marriage disintegration when children leave home, but different studies suggest couples are likely to become closer. A woman's self-esteem falls at this time; a woman's self-esteem rises at this time. The empty nest syndrome is a myth; the empty nest is a stressful time for women. So surrounded by research papers, sociology books and with an aching brain, I decided to leave the academics out of it.

It was a relief to find that the confusion was not just mine. In 1979 gerontologists Troll, Miller and Atchley observed that the family literature abounds with contradictory statements about empty nest syndrome and about marital relationships at this stage. There is an apparent peak in divorce rates around this time, yet demographic data shows no such peak and many couples report a time of 'second honeymoon'. Such inconsistency in the research would suggest that this experience is highly individual and subjective and that its effects are too diverse to be accurately measured by scientific methods of research.

This book is not searching for empirical proof and in fact the contradictory research would suggest that there *is* no such proof. What it seeks to do is to provide a forum for women to share their feelings and experiences and for other women to be able to identify with them.

A few of the women who wrote to me also did not believe in the concept of empty nest, but their letters clearly illustrate that each person's experience, when it happens, is both subjective and unpredictable.

Ruth wrote:

> I feel that women have been conditioned to experience
> desolation when their children leave. But there is a lot of the
> animal in us – kittens leave and I don't think the mother cat
> suffers – I've always had cats.
>
> I found it a relief when the third child left – I loved them and
> still do but the generations no longer matched. They needed
> new and wider experiences, we needed more quiet. Many
> women feel as I do. Those almost-grown-ups can be trying.
> You miss them, yes, but you don't grieve. Who invented the
> idea of the 'empty nest' anyway? It's modern.

People often talk of the empty nest syndrome as being peculiar to
humans and therefore not 'natural'. In fact, it can be seen in many
species of animals. I have had a number of cat mothers and
observed that like women, cats are all different in their mothering. I have had some who have obviously breathed a sigh of
relief when their kittens went, or who stopped fussing over them
as soon as they started on solid food. On the other hand, I have
had cats who have wanted to go on feeding their kittens long after
the kittens would rather play than suckle. As for leaving home,
some appeared not to notice that six or so of their children had
disappeared in a couple of days while others have been severely
and obviously distressed. It has been necessary with these cats to
let the kittens go in stages and even then, the mothers have
grieved when the last one went. One cat used to fetch socks from
upstairs when her final kitten left and carry them around for days,
crying all the time. It is a myth that animals don't have empty
nests. Indeed, it is very common for cats to go straight out and
get pregnant again when their kittens go, so strong is the instinct
to procreate.

While we on the whole do not behave in this way – though
many women, seeing their children growing up decide to have a
late baby or two – it is worth noting that planning our families
relies on expedience and a host of practical and social considerations. We are not ruled by the biological instinct to continue to
bear children until the menopause, though somewhere inside us,

overlaid by twentieth century ways of life, those instincts still lie deeply hidden.

This brings me to Ruth's second point that the empty nest is a modern concept. She's right, but not because we have been conditioned to feel this way. The modern, nuclear family has created an artificial hiatus in the natural continuum of the passage of parent to grandparent. When families were larger, the eldest would be producing their own offspring while the youngest children would still be at home. This ensured a smooth transition without the long gap of years that tends to occur now between the leaving of the last child and the birth of the first grandchild. The women who talked about their empty nests had strong feelings about grandchildren. Those who had them found it a wonderfully fulfilling experience, a new phase, children to love and to share lives with without the responsibility of being a parent. Many who had not reached that stage said how much they were looking forward to it.

Dr Jill Welbourne, a psychiatrist at the Bristol Royal Infirmary told me:

> The people I see who suffer from the empty nest syndrome have too long a gap between kids leaving home and grandchildren being produced. I don't think we're designed to live in small, nuclear family clutches, I think human beings are basically tribal and the kind of unit that feels OK is anywhere between six and 25.

In addition, women with large families are more likely to extend their period of childbearing so that their last child leaves home when they are well into their sixties. For some reason, probably biological, post-menopausal empty nests seem to cause very much less trauma. Many women report an overwhelming urge to have another baby at the age of about 40.

It happened to me and though I decided against it for a number of reasons, the biological and emotional drive to do so was almost overpowering. At that time my children were nowhere near the age of leaving home and the prospect of empty nest had not crossed my mind. As Susi wrote:

I don't feel ready for this. I keep wishing I'd had more children and I can't stop brooding on this. I did have two miscarriages after our last child and decided then not to continue trying in case there might be something wrong with the babies I was conceiving – I was 38 then. Now I keep looking at small children and remembering mine at that age and thinking that if I had succeeded in having another one it would be 10 now, giving me eight more years with one at home. I look at my sister who is 43 and who has two children, one six and one two, and I think how lucky she is to have all those years with them ahead of her. I don't talk about this – people think you can't let go of your children and that you are being self-indulgent.

It makes me think of the wonderfully outrageous Caitlin Thomas, wife of Dylan Thomas, who defied convention in every area of her life and cocked a final snook at boring British social mores by having a baby with her Italian partner when she was 49.

Of course, this can still be seen with large families where the mother has given birth in her forties. I know women who have the comforting cycle of grandchildren coming to visit and a child or two still at home. Novelists Fay Weldon and Alice Thomas Ellis are both in their sixties with grandchildren coming and going and a child at home still. Neither anticipates a painful empty nest. I am sure that some women will be reading this with indignation at the suggestion that the only way to avoid empty nest syndrome is to procreate as our grandmothers did, so I must be clear here. It is not the only way – I am just explaining the point that this is why the empty nest is a relatively modern state of affairs.

The other major change in family life, especially among the middle classes, is the loss of the extended family. At one time, children did not move away, they lived, worked and married in the district where their parents and grandparents had been. The kind of mobility and separation that occurs now, largely due to employment necessities and opportunities, means that families are scattered. The inner city slum clearances of the 1960s and 1970s were seen as altogether good, but families who had taken for granted the security of proximity were torn apart and for the

first time generations and lateral family extensions found themselves in another part of the city or even the country.

Empty nest syndrome is not only a modern concept, it is also a
particularly English one. My own children are the first generation
in my family to leave in this way. I am Welsh and the clannish practice of staying in the same area as the rest of the family was deeply
ingrained. It would never have occurred to me to move away
from my parents and in fact, when we did move to another part of
the country, we found accommodation for them, too. On the
other hand, neither my husband nor his parents would have
considered such a thing; when we got married, they made it very
clear that he was now on his own. My ethnic roots are simply
different from his.

While researching this book, I received a phone call from a
woman in her sixties who had heard I was writing about empty
nest syndrome. Her children had scattered far and wide and what
she was finding hard was being an Englishwoman living in Wales.
'I feel so envious of the women round here,' she told me. 'Their
children all go to local universities and come home at weekends.
Then, more often than not, they stay in the same area to find
work and often end up marrying and living locally.' This was all
completely familiar to me; in my family, living in Wales meant that
if you went to university you went to Swansea, just down the
road. In England, children make a point of choosing a university
a good distance away from home. My daughters were told by
their school to apply only to universities at least 100 miles away
from home so that they would not be tempted to come back for
weekends, nor their parents to visit them. This suggests a
misreading of parents' motives by the school; an assumption that
they will not be able to let their children go. In the event, unless
the university was chosen for a particular degree course, this
policy tended to result in great expense for students when they
did want to visit, or come home in vacations.

Julia, an Englishwoman living in Italy, wrote of her own
response to her children leaving and of the cultural differences
there:

| Our children were always brought up to be independent and

do for themselves and help with the chores – something almost unheard of in this very mother-orientated society. When our elder girl went to England to study, aged 18, it was assumed that she would live with relatives. I missed her a lot as she was a homebody and so better company than the other two, but it was bearable. Then out of the blue our second daughter decided that she too was going to England to study. We were pleased as we have always encouraged our children to choose what they want to do, so after the summer both girls left. At first I thought I was just missing them but I soon realized that I was prey to the empty nest syndrome even though I still had a child at home.

It was really terrible and was made much worse by the fact that none of my Italian friends would even let their children go and study in towns 30 kilometres away let alone across the sea. Also I had not imagined that I would be like this as I'd always been a letting-go sort of mother. Our elder girl is home again and it is wonderful having her. When she leaves, as one day she will, I don't know how I shall cope. So I tell her that however much I lean on her or her sister, they must push me off and get on with their own lives.

SHE magazine, (December 1993), looked at the idea of the extended family today, showing ethnic and demographic differences. Carole, married with three children, lives in Cardiff where her job with Welsh National Opera had taken her. She subsequently met her husband there and so it became home. Her mother and grandmother are still in Yorkshire where she grew up. Carole does see her mother regularly but what she misses is 'the intimacy, the day-to-day closeness you have when you live near your family'.

Carole's mother Nancy is still living three miles from where she was born and two-and-a-half from her own mother. Having her own mother close by was, she says, security when her children were young – 'I could always call on her.' But, she says, life is different now and women's expectations are different too; 'Mothers today don't put as much pressure on their children. I wouldn't expect my children to be at my beck and call as much as my mother expects me to be.'

And Nancy's mother, Sarah, comments on the differences, when children no longer grow up with family all around them, always an aunt or a granny to go to:

> Life is altogether different now. There is far more freedom and children move away. People have to go where the work is. You have to let them go.

In the same article, a West Indian mother and daughter talk about family ties. Daughter Pam says that having a grandchild was very important for her mother – it was extending the family. While Pam goes out to work, her mother Cynthia, 71, looks after Kyle. There is no question of childcare. 'She would be very upset if I sent him to a childminder,' says Pam. Every night, when Pam collects Kyle, her mother always has a meal ready for her. Cynthia's role as a mother is still paramount in their lives.

Both Asian and Afro-Caribbean families have a tradition of staying together – an issue which the ever topical series *The Archers* on Radio Four has tackled by introducing to Ambridge an independent-minded Asian woman lawyer whose family are forever trying to get her to return to them – they all live together in another part of the country. Empty nest grieving, depression and bewilderment have been found to deeply affect black and coloured women whose British-born children adopt the modern customs of this country and leave home, especially if they marry and set up home in a different part of the country.

Also compare the family bonds of other cultures to the English practice of sending children to boarding school. This effectively means handing over the upbringing of the child to strangers at the age of six or nine or 11 – many people believe the younger the better. Am I perverse in being unable to understand the logic which says that trained teachers and institutional care produce a better adult than a loving family home? Do people really believe that the qualities and values which will be instilled into their children by strangers must be better than they, as parents, can offer? It seems to me an extraordinary concept, though I know there are situations when boarding school can give a child more stability than a chaotic or insecure home life.

As Penelope Leach says in her book *Children First*:

> The less time parents and children spend together, and the
> fewer thoughts and activities they share, the more powerful
> secondary influences are likely to be. Growing, developing
> changing children cannot be left on ice when parents are not
> around, so time and space in minds and hearts get filled by
> other people.

My husband, who was sent to boarding school at the relatively
advanced age of nine, remembers wondering if he would ever see
his parents again. What does this do to women, whose nests are
effectively emptied when their children are still infants? Even
though they come home for holidays, the major part of their time
is spent away from home, rather like going to university. I talked
to women whose children are, or were at boarding schools and
got a variety of responses:

> My husband's family all went to boarding school and he
> insisted that our two boys carry on the tradition. They are nine
> and 12 now and I don't think I will ever stop missing them.
> They have gone. They have actually left home. My biggest
> regret is that I didn't stand up to my husband and try and
> refuse to let them go, but I am much younger than him and he
> is a bit of a bully. Empty nest? My nest has been empty since
> the second one went to school two years ago.

> Where I live (Surrey), most people send their children to
> boarding school. There's a pattern we all follow – pre-prep
> until the age of seven, then either day or boarding prep school,
> then public school. When they are still at home, they're being
> prepared all the time. They go to the right out-of-school
> activities, they're taught not to cry, to keep a stiff upper lip, all
> that stuff. This is not my background and quite frankly I find it
> amazing and appalling. My son is in his first term at boarding
> school, he's 11, and I'm trying to persuade my husband to let
> him come home and attend day school. It's a fight, though and
> I'm not sure I'm going to win.

I believed boarding school was the right thing for my children. We took our son to his prep school last year when he was seven. I will always be haunted by the memory of leaving him, crying his eyes out, clutching his teddy, absolutely unable to believe that we were leaving him. Now he has got used to it, but I can't help wondering whether in that process his spirit was broken. And holidays are dreadful because he settles at home then cries for about a week before he's due to go back. He begs me to keep him at home and I don't know what to do. I'm missing his growing up, his development as a person and I'm beginning to think this is all wrong.

I've got used to them being away and it does mean I can get on with my own life. They do come home for holidays, you know. And boarding school gives them the best possible education and preparation for life.

What a mixture of convictions and emotions. Many of those women were torn apart, yet belonged to a social class where boarding school was regarded as such a normal process that they felt diffident about admitting their feelings of loss. And surely, for a child to leave home at the age of seven, or even 13, it is a great and premature loss, an untimely and unnatural empty nest. It seems though that parents now are having second thoughts about this peculiar practice; in February 1995, a report from the Independent Schools Information Service (ISIS) disclosed that there has been a sharp decline in the number of parents who choose to send their children to boarding school. In the preceding two years, boarding pupils had fallen by an eighth, due, says the report, not to financial strictures but to the fact that today's parents are becoming increasingly unwilling to send their children away, especially at an early age. John Rae, ex-headmaster of Westminster School, who has his ear to the ground in matters educational reports that 'Once-famous brand names are no longer a guarantee of quality. Some boarding schools are so short of pupils they can no longer attract good staff.' (*The Times*, 20.2.95)

While ISIS, an organization for the support and promotion of independent and boarding schools bemoans this state of affairs, which is leading to schools having to close, I cannot sympathize with the organization or the schools. I think of those children enjoying their birthright of home and parenting and of those mothers whose nest will not be emptied prematurely and I rejoice. Social factors are peculiarly potent and I believe that this change can only be for the good.

However, there are times when difficult decisions have to be made – when a child's education suffers from constant moving about, when parents are in the Services for instance; times when a parent believes that the emotional development of a child may be hindered by staying at home. The choice of boarding school is made for the child's sake, though it costs the mother dearly. Phyllis had to make such a decision:

> My husband was in the RAF and due to our moving about so often we decided that our son's education was suffering. We therefore sent him to boarding school and that was my first experience of suffering the loss of one of my children. I missed him so much that I became anorexic and had a nervous breakdown, even though he was enjoying every minute of it.

And so did Margaret:

> My husband died when Tim was only 11 years old and I had a big decision to make. I knew I could not be selfish and keep him home with me. I had only one son and I did not want him to become a 'mother's boy', so I sent him to boarding school in Oxfordshire. I missed him terribly of course, but I had him home during the holidays. He has always thanked me for not being possessive and, a bonus for me, we are really good friends. He has always been so thoughtful and even though he is now 33, he phones every week and often comes to stay for two or three days. He still has many friends in this area as it is where he lived as a schoolboy – another pleasure for him. It was very hard at the time but I believe I made the right decision.

Feminism: Ally or Enemy?

Another major influence has been feminism, and while it has liberated us, I feel it has also denied us the right to grieve for what is, for most women, a major loss and an important transition, a rite of passage that needs marking in some way. This letter, from Judith, shows how feminist conditioning can catch us out:

> Nowadays it seems that I have a secret. Something I feel ashamed about at any rate, something which appalls me. It concerns my son, Tom, who is 20. He left home recently to go to university – and I just cannot seem to live without him.
>
> You'd be surprised if you knew me because I don't seem the type to say that sort of thing. I've got plenty of interests, friends, hobbies. I'm mad about opera, travel, I read a lot. I've always been quite militant about overcoming outmoded notions of femininity and motherhood. I've been on marches, visited Greenham, worked on a women's peace project. What's wrong with me? How can I suffer from something I don't believe in – the empty nest syndrome?

But the exhortation to be someone in your own right, while completely valid, can have its down side, as expressed in Judith's letter. Why should she feel 'appalled' and 'ashamed'? Why should she feel that her grieving must be a secret? Her letter shows her to be a feminist and it would seem that her feminist determination has visited upon her a sense of guilt and failure, whereas what she is experiencing is normal.

What feminism is overlooking in this arena is that there has to be an end before there can be a beginning. Judith is far from the only woman to express shame or guilt about her feelings of grief. But in trying to toe the feminist party line we can be pressured, and duped too, into feeling we must leap from caring for our children into being third age Superwoman.

Talking to women in their sixties and seventies who have been on the whole untouched by feminism, I found that they had a sisterhood of their own. The time when their children left was acknowledged as a time to mourn. They found nothing strange or unnatural in that. They were not plagued by feelings of guilt or accusations that they were living through their children. They bonded with other women undergoing the same process – and they came through it and moved on. Gerry, mother of four remembers the day her last child left:

> We took her to college and saw her settled in, then went home. When we got inside the house and felt its emptiness we both sat down and cried our eyes out.

Gerry is one of the most fulfilled women I know. Since her children left home she has had a satisfying job, taken an honours degree and filled her time enjoyably and productively. Now a widow and a grandmother, she still has more interests and friends than she can find time for. She sees her children, who are scattered, at regular intervals and feels the balance of her life is right. She is a very contented woman. But she took time to pass from one stage to another, just as is necessary with any bereavement.

We are lucky that it is now widely acknowledged that the third age, post-50, post-menopause and post-child-rearing is not the end. Indeed it is the beginning of an entirely new phase for women in which we can do anything we want to. Fifty used to be considered old, 'past it' – what a contrast to the fifty-plus women of today.

When Joyce Hopkirk launched *Chic*, her new magazine for older women, in early 1994, she was quoted as 'feeling passionately that ours is the first time in the history of the world that women in their forties and fifties have been so resourceful, dynamic and, well, young'. She says:

> My mother's generation were old women at 50, today we are taking university degrees, setting up our own companies, backpacking across Australia. I certainly don't think of Joanna Lumley, Marie Helvin, Julie Christie, Anna Ford and hundreds more sexy, gorgeous 40-somethings as grey-haired old ladies. The idea is hilarious.

Chic's chief selling point is 'to encourage women to tackle new challenges'. A Fresh Start section is 'packed with ideas to interest empty nesters'. Hopkirk says:

> It is when the children and their sticky fingers have gone that many women get excited about sprucing up the decor. It is these women who have the dosh, too. (*Daily Mail*, 3.5.94)

Alright, so no one in their right mind would deny that the opportunities are there for us. But Hopkirk and *Chic* are too aspirational for the average woman who may not be able – or even want – to identify with Joanna Lumley, Marie Helvin *et al*. There is tremendous pressure here to be 'resourceful, dynamic and young' – get rid of the children, travel, take a degree, set up a company. Empty nest? Grieving? Loss? What's that? As for the assertion that at our age we are the ones with the money this is only true for a certain middle-class group of women.

We are pushed from all sides. A friend directed me to a section in Susan Jeffers' book *Feel the Fear and Do It Anyway* – a book I knew and admired. This extract tells the story of a woman who said goodbye to her son when he went off to college:

> With tears in her eyes, she watched him walk down the path to his new car, knowing he would return again only as a visitor. It was not time to let him go. She reported thinking, yes, this is the way life is . . . always changing. Things don't last forever. She let herself cry for a while, but soon picked herself up and decided to prepare a candlelit dinner. After all, she and her husband would be alone for the first time in many years, so she was determined to make a honeymoon of it.

Jeffers contrasts this with the parent who dreads her children leaving home, and when it finally happens is able to see only the emptiness of the house and the uselessness of her life. 'Such a person, resisting change, misses the new pathways opening up for her,' she writes. 'There is something enriching about leaving one beautiful experience in your life and looking forward to other beautiful experiences.'

My friend wrote:

This is probably true, but surely there is a grieving process?
And finding the next beautiful thing isn't easy!

Jeffers is, of course, right about moving on. But she is too glib at this point. The leap from tearful goodbyes to candlelit, honeymoon dinner does not really ring true for the average, emotional woman. And I strongly dislike the sense of blame implied in the case of the parent who does not immediately move on to the next beautiful thing. There have to be silences and spaces between the different phases of development in our lives, not a frenetic rush from one experience to another. I think the friend who highlighted this is right.

If there is to be any understanding, any sense of real sisterhood among women, we have to accept that the time when children leave home is a highly individual experience for each person. The experiences of the women in this book range from real grief, with all its accompanying emotions, to a time of resolution where they have found different roles and with them, learned to be mothers to adults.

Why Do We Have Children?

Why do we have children? An almost impossible question with no definitive answer. Asking a handful of women produces a varied crop of answers:

I always knew I wanted children, but I would find it very difficult to put into words why I did.

I can remember standing in the school playground when I was about five and watching my teacher talking to a group of children. I was completely overwhelmed with a longing to grow up and have children of my own. It lasted as strongly as that until I was about 15, then it disappeared. But when I was married the longing returned and it was every bit as overwhelming.

My mother used to plait my hair for school every morning – I

suppose I was about eight. It was a little ritual I enjoyed
tremendously – I think it was the closeness and familiarity of it.
I remember thinking to myself one day that it must be lovely to
be a Mummy – and from that moment I knew I wanted
children.

I took it for granted, you know, university, job, marriage,
children – I never thought about why.

Maternal instinct – nothing rational, just overwhelming.

I come from a big family and could not imagine just being a
couple – having children seemed natural.

To please my mother, to please his mother, to please society, I
suppose.

Oh, I don't know, you just do, don't you? It's part of being a
woman, isn't it?

I had always wanted to experience everything I possibly could
in life. I took all the opportunities that came my way. I wanted
to get into Oxford and I did, I wanted a career in publishing
and I have that. I have had all kinds of relationships, gay and
straight. When I had been settled with my partner for five
years, by which time I was 34, I wanted the experience of
having a child, so I had one. I want to try everything that is
possible for a woman to do.

I do not think women nowadays think any more deeply about all
the implications of having children than did other generations,
even though pregnancy appears to be more carefully planned to
fit in with careers, finance, etc. The biological urge is extremely
strong and usually overcomes other resistances. We do I believe,
think very carefully about what it will mean to have a baby. We
consider its impact on all aspects of our lives but it is very difficult
to see ourselves with a growing family.

Whatever our original reasons for becoming mothers, the truth is that many women find motherhood the single most fulfilling, most rewarding, most enjoyable thing they have ever done. And because we don't analyse why we have children – and it would be a fairly unnatural, even clinical thing to do – the time when they leave home can be hedged about with another kind of guilt, as expressed by Ruth:

> I guess there is a sort of guilt tied up with all this – the apron strings must be loosed, but there may even be a fear of loss of purpose and usefulness – which is then again visited by guilt; after all, one does not have children in order to be useful!

The fact is that we have children in order to lose them. As Virginia Ironside puts it:

> The very job of mothering contains, if successfully carried out, a self-destruct device that explodes in her face 20 years on. (*The Independent*, 14.9.93)

There is a common misconception that empty nest sufferers are the women who have subjugated their own lives, their careers, their interests to the bringing up of children. Even some experts make the mistake of assuming that it is the woman who devotes herself to *Kinder, Küche, Kirche* who will find it hardest when the children leave. In an interview on Southern Counties Radio on 21 January 1995, Dr Bernice Andrews of London University, who has conducted research in the area of women and depression, spoke of the empty nest syndrome: 'It may be that for women for whom the children and their home is their whole focus that it is quite likely that there is this tremendous hole when the children leave.' But the 'tremendous hole' is not the result of lack of activity or interests, as Margaret pointed out: 'When children leave home, the suggestion is made that the woman has the chance of a new life. The thing is that I have always done a lot of terribly interesting things, my husband and I taking it in turns to look after the children. So, for me, when they left home I was bereft because it was a *psychological* loss, which could not be filled with more activity or thought.'

Equally, the women who have given home and family that kind of concentrated devotion over a period of many years may be quite ready to move into a different phase of their lives when their children leave. I remember one woman who had children at the same time as I did. She left the job she enjoyed and was a *real* housewife and mother. She did her housework *every* day. She cooked home-made steak and kidney puddings and apple pies and trifles. She made curtains for the home, re-covered upholstery and made her children's clothes. From the very start, she stimulated her babies' interests, sticking coloured pictures round their prams, making them mobiles, giving them differently textured objects to try out. When they got to pre-school age, she painstakingly made flash cards and stuck them to everything in the house. And when they got older and watched *Blue Peter*, she always had sticky-backed plastic to hand, while I cringed and dreaded my children asking if they could make whatever ingenious creation was on display that week. She was concerned when I went back to work when my youngest was six. 'Are you sure the family aren't suffering?' she asked me. Her children never had to wash their own clothes or get supper when they were teenagers. Her husband always had beautifully ironed shirts and wasn't reduced to wearing creased ones from the clean washing basket or dirty ones from the day before. And so it continued. When her children left home, she shed a brief tear for the end of an era, then went out, got herself a good job, immersed herself in a busy social life and never suffered empty nest pangs.

The way we face our own empty nests has its roots in our own childhood experiences of family. A secure childhood, one in which a person knows love and relative freedom from major disruption, provides a bedrock of certainty that life is somehow safe, that the people we love who leave us will come back – and at a deeply unconscious level, that they are not necessary to our survival. The point is that empty nest feelings are unpredictable. I think it is no coincidence that the woman I have been describing had a particularly happy and secure childhood in which she felt loved, wanted and important.

In the research I conducted amongst women suffering empty nest syndrome I found no correlation between the depth of suffering and the existence of interests, career, friends and social life in each woman's life. Most spoke of having good personal relationships with a partner and/or with friends and in fact many expressed bewilderment that they should feel such pain when their lives were so full of other things. The following account is fairly typical:

> I've worked since my youngest child was 11 and I love my job. I love the stimulus of adult company during the day, I enjoy the sharing, the fun, the drink at the pub at lunchtime. I've made good friends there – and always, when I got home, there were the children, wanting to tell me about their day, having friends round for supper, practising their music, lying around in front of the television, even listening to me talking about my day. Now that they've grown up and left home, I still have my super job and all that goes with it. Why then, do I feel such a gap, such a blank in my busy, fulfilled life? I never thought it could happen to me.

Cilla Black, one of the nation's best-loved entertainers, and acclaimed actresses Anne Bancroft and Jane Lapotaire are three famous and successful women with the high profile lives that many might envy and of whom it would probably be assumed that empty nest syndrome would have no place in their thoughts. These women all have clearly defined roles, other than mother-hood, and their roles are endorsed by an enormous amount of public recognition. Yet all three have suffered badly, proving that no amount of satisfying and enriching work is insurance against these feelings.

In the midst of a hectic recording schedule, doing work she loved, Cilla Black appeared on daytime television to talk about the way she felt. With much emotion, she frankly and openly described how much she missed her two older sons, both of whom had left home and how much she was dreading the coming autumn when her 12-year-old was off to boarding school. Some months later, *The Sun* newspaper reported an interview that had taken place on BBC Radio Wales between Cilla and Falklands war veteran Simon Weston. In an article entitled *My lonely plight, by TV*

Cilla, Victor Chapple wrote that Cilla 'confessed she feels very lonely now her three sons have left home. The TV hostess said she was tempted to give up fame and fortune and return to her old life in Liverpool.' The report went on to say that Cilla, who lives in a 10 bedroomed mansion said 'It's a big house and I'm very lonely. It would not bother me in the least if I lost everything. I'm desperately trying to get back to that two-up, two-down cottage kind of home-like existence. It was total happiness and a laugh a minute.'

Successful actress Anne Bancroft is poised, sophisticated and apparently confident. She is happily married to another hugely successful actor, Mel Brooks. But success has not been important to Anne Bancroft; home and family have always come first. In an interview with Andrew Duncan (*Radio Times* 16.11.94) she reveals that she went into therapy to try to help her cope with the loss she felt when her son, Max, left home. She says:

> I found myself tearful so much of the time. What tears mothers apart is they lose their main job, which is to help. It's painful to let children go into this dangerous, dangerous world and I'm still finding it so . . . Think of the bird kicking the baby out of the nest. I don't think birds feel as conflicted as I did though.

Jane Lapotaire brought up her son, Rowan, entirely on her own with no back-up support when she and his father parted when Rowan was five. Their bond is understandably very strong. Though she has had a brilliantly successful acting career she made sacrifices for her son. After playing Joy Davidman in the play *Shadowlands* to great critical acclaim, she decided not to go with the play to Broadway because Rowan was preparing for Oxford entrance and she wanted to be there for him while he studied. In spite of the offers of work that continued to pour in, Jane went through a period of extreme grief when Rowan left:

> He'd been the centre of my life for so long that I spent six months feeling really bereaved because he'd grown up and left school. It was the end of being Mum but I had to let him go. I'd never want to load him with guilt, to say 'after all I've done for you'. I want to give him unconditional love.

Women often have high expectations of themselves and since our culture puts the emphasis on the necessity of letting children go, many are surprised that they do react in this way, especially when they have filled their lives with other activities and interests. But as agony aunt Gill Cox said to a group of mothers discussing empty nest syndrome:

> This is a bit like a bereavement for some people and it takes time to work through that. It helps if you've got your own life but I don't think it completely takes the pain away.

Could we have prepared for this, while deeply involved with small children growing up? Jill Welbourne thinks so:

> Just as you have to start training a child for adult independence when it's about three, by saying 'Do you want your egg poached or scrambled?' or 'Are you going to wear your mackintosh or your coat?' so that within its limits the child is practising – you don't suddenly become able to choose for yourself because you've hit 18 – so in exactly the same way you start thinking about what you do when the kids have left home somewhere on the way home from the maternity hospital.

A counsel of perfection and one that few mothers would think of. The time when we can perhaps begin to prepare is the teenage years, when, though still living at home, our children begin to assert their separateness, often in the form of rebellion and often by absenting themselves, either for long periods in their rooms, or being out with friends. Looking back, I realize that it was a rehearsal for the final leaving – they are with you but somehow not among you, but it is hard to imagine the silence, the absence of vitality, when they are gone.

As one friend said:

> When they were babies I couldn't imagine them going to school, and when they did, I couldn't imagine them at secondary school, or university – and so it went on. You live in

the present – you can't project forward and think of how it will be when they are grown up.

As mothers of grown children we know too well how fast their childhoods pass. When I think of my 23-year-old daughter in America, my 20-year-old at university and my 17-year-old on the brink of adulthood, I cannot believe that so many years have passed since I left hospital with a brand-new carrycot for the first time. I do not think I had an awareness of the years rushing by – I was too busy getting on with the present. I remember a photograph of my son when he was about ten – by some trick of the camera, or his expression in that moment, you could clearly see how he would look when he was much older – and he does. I recall trying to picture a 16- or 17-year-old – but I couldn't because the reality was that I had a ten-year-old.

What we can do is to tell mothers of young children to make the very most of their childhoods. It is easy when coping with toddler tantrums or pre-pubescent sulks to wish you were onto the next phase and in doing so, to miss the reality of the present. I said this to a friend with a five-year-old and a nine-year-old recently and she thought about it carefully and thanked me. She said she was glad someone had told her. It has made a difference to the way she looks at her children, deliberately holding pictures of them in her mind with a heightened awareness of the passage of time.

And so because it is almost impossible to project forward, it is natural when the time of leaving comes to find ourselves looking back before we are ready to move on.

3 WHO SUFFERS FROM EMPTY NEST SYNDROME?

Nobody can claim to be invulnerable to the often unpredictable and unexpected emotions surrounding the time when our children leave home. Fathers as well as mothers can be affected, though on the whole less frequently and less intensely. It can afflict women who are quite sure that it will not happen to them, who have a very clear idea of what motherhood means. Many women I have spoken to admitted that the feelings accompanying the ending of this phase of their motherhood took them completely by surprise. Difficulty making this transition does not apply to every woman though; in fact there is no immediate or obvious explanation as to why it should affect some women and not others. But there are reasons for this and it may be useful to look at some of them.

When I had collated the 200 or so accounts of women's feelings about their children leaving home, I found myself asking several questions. What sort of women suffered empty nest syndrome? Why did it seem like a smooth passage for some, while others were devastated? Why did so many women talk about feeling bereaved? Why did they feel that their life no longer had any purpose? And conversely, why did this same life event make some women feel that a new era was opening up for them, causing feelings of excitement without any accompanying grief other than perhaps a transient sadness of the kind that accompanies any such passing? I realized that the central feature of this was loss. But why was it not consistent, in the way it is if, for instance, a child dies – a universally recognized tragedy that all mothers can identify with?

There were no obvious answers. There was no pattern; there were women who had worked, those who had stayed at home, those who had done something else outside the home, like voluntary work. There were single women and women with happy, loving relationships with husbands or partners. It was impossible to pin it down to categories – it was completely random. So there must, I thought, be other factors at play here. I asked two extremely wise and experienced women about this. Tirril Harris is a psychologist and psychotherapist, a research fellow at London University. Ruth Young is a psychotherapist. I knew both these women would have the knowledge and wisdom to unlock this puzzle for me, and they did.

I outlined a case history to Ruth. This was a woman who had outwardly succeeded in all aspects of her life. She is a fairly well-known public figure with a satisfying and successful career. She has a strong personality and her self-esteem is high – at least in the context of her outer world. And she has a husband she loves. Yet she suffered a major depression when her children left home. A year after the event, she seems no nearer to coming to terms with her loss. During that year her career received a major boost, but it means little to her. 'I'd give it up', she said, 'if I could turn the clock back and have them around, with their friends, drinking endless cups of coffee and talking and talking while I cook them all a huge meal and enjoy their company.'

Ruth said:

The woman who enjoys making a meal for a dozen young people needs to ask who she is doing it for. Would working in a soup kitchen, for instance, fulfil the same role? It could be more to do with identifying as a good mother than with the children's need. For some women this may be the *only* sort of thing which enables or allows them to feel good about themselves – it affirms them, it is a way of *being* somebody, where one is affirmed as having a reason for living, for actually *existing* at all. When I think about what it is that is missing for people who have difficulty shifting from one stage to another, I keep coming back to the word 'affirming'. It comes from a great sense that unless they are needed by somebody, they have no being and no right to be. I think that stems from being a very small child. If, at that stage, you constantly get the sense that you're exactly what everyone was looking for and you're lovely, and they're all really happy to have you, then I think those people never have any difficulty in shifting from stage to stage because there is something within them that goes with them, no matter what. And where they are isn't really relevant to who they are, to their existence. They are not dependent on other people's need for them or on needing someone themselves. Obviously there are times when they are happy to be there for somebody else but their *existence* doesn't depend on it, their reality doesn't depend on it.

This made me think of the Russian poet, Irina Ratushinskaya, who was imprisoned in the Ukraine for writing poetry. Something she said in a radio interview had remained in my mind. She was talking about memories of her childhood when she had lived with her parents and family in a single room in a communal flat. Her parents always made a point of celebrating her birthdays, giving her presents and inviting her friends in. This was very unpopular with the neighbours because of their close proximity and the noise created by a group of young people in a confined area. There were many protests from the neighbours, she said, but her parents always dealt with these and made sure that the birthdays were always honoured in this way. She said: 'This made me feel as if I was a very important person'. When she spoke of her imprisonment she said 'I didn't think I would survive prison because I suffer so much from claustrophobia'. Yet not only did she survive, she continued to write while in a labour camp, smuggling her poems out via certain trusted guards, risking her life for her passionate convictions. In the context of what Ruth had been saying, I felt that the sense Irina's parents had given her of being 'a very important person' must have gone a long way to shaping the indomitable spirit that was later to endure so much and yet to produce that brave and wonderful output of poetry in such dangerous conditions. Those who cope well with life and adversity, those who 'pull themselves up by their bootstraps' and appear competent and resolute in crisis are much admired. But it should not be forgotten that those who seem to go under, who need help, who seem weak in the eyes of the world may well never have had a childhood where they were given a sense that they were important, and where their existence enhanced the lives of those around them. But is this sort of security not fairly rare? I asked Ruth.

> I don't think it's as rare as you might expect it to be. When you think of us with our very odd sort of childhood (Ruth and her sister had no real home base after their mother died when Ruth was six) – we never had that sense that we only existed if we were what other people wanted. I can only suppose that my six years were enough to give me that security. This is one of the reasons that I do think that if women can stay with their children until they are four at the very earliest, it doesn't much matter what happens after that, but it's this awful business of losing Mum at six months and then having no continuity of seeing oneself reflected in the same pair of eyes until you feel that somehow, you're there.
>
> It seems to me that when people lose themselves after their children leave home, one needs to ask one fundamental question – why they have so little sense of their own identity? What was their sense of identity when they were children; who did they *feel* they were? I think it is people who have never had that solid sense of identity who therefore are constantly seeking to be the centre of attention. I do not mean that disparagingly, I mean in the sense of the person who is needed. It's a sense of being OK, no matter what. The security is very hard to define but it's at the heart of all of this. Nothing can shift it once it's there.

I reminded Ruth of a mutual acquaintance who had had such a devastatingly insecure and unhappy childhood that she changed her name at the age of 21 when she got married as a deliberate symbolic gesture of leaving her past behind and to start afresh with a new identity. Ruth said:

> And she built up that identity through her marriage and

children. Now that the children have left, that's been taken away too and she's got to rebuild another identity.

Women who suffer badly from empty nest syndrome are often super-conscientious mothers. One wonders what triggered this need to get it all right. There's been a fairly severe wound, early in their lives at some time and it's that wound that's opened now. I do think this early wounding is the heart of the difference between women who suffer and those who don't, I really believe that. From all I have ever read and heard from people whose wisdom and opinions I respect, that certainly seems to be the case.

Ruth also mentioned Konrad Lorenz' famous imprinting experiments where ducklings who saw a human being before they saw their mothers would follow and try and copy that person; the human had imprinted himself ineradicably in the ducklings' mind as the parent figure.

There is that crucial moment with us, inside us, and if we miss that somehow, we go off on the wrong track.

So if we miss it, I asked, do we unconsciously use our children to replace that experience?

I don't doubt that at all. I think we mother them in lieu of having been mothered, a sort of vicarious thing. There is a sense in which one's own neglected inner child is being mothered as well through the mothering of our children. It throws you right back to your own beginning, that time when that channel (being mothered) was closed.

If women had lacked adequate mothering, I suggested to Ruth, was it likely that they also missed a sense of family? Might having their own children cause them to try to create the family they had never had?

I do think so, yes. Every time I thought round this I came up with the same thing – that of somehow trying to make up for something that one's instincts know one needs, even if one's head doesn't.

If that is the case, I said, and deprived women have successfully created a family, why is 20 or so years of it not enough to stop the pain they feel when children leave?

It isn't so much a question of making up for what you never had, it's what that would have *given* you, and that is identity, a sense of self, of ego, if you like, a sense of actually existing in your own right without any reference to who is there and who is not there. You can't make up for it. But you can learn to find it for yourself at that point.

When I asked Tirril Harris the fundamental question 'Why?' she, too emphasized the importance of the mother's own experience of being mothered:

The quality of mothering is vital. Good early mothering gets into one's soul and gives one a lasting resilience. This kind of mothering teaches children how to cope with life and that stays with them forever. It's the absence of mothering that makes people vulnerable to stressful life events, not just the absence of mother. If this early mothering does not take place, a woman's own mothering role gets invested with making up what she never had. She wants that wonderful moment when two people succeed in producing comfort for each other, because she was deprived of that when she was little. And you can get great comfort from providing comfort for children. So a great deal is dependent on what happened to the mother when she was young. If she had a deprived childhood emotionally, she will be vulnerable with her own children and will possibly suffer greatly when they leave home because she has invested so much in the mother role.

This was beginning to make sense to me. Of the women I questioned those who were suffering greatly had indeed consistently missed a sense of being wanted, being mothered. Some, whose mothers are still alive, have difficult and ambivalent feelings about them. There were two women in particular, for whom I would have expected the empty nest to be a traumatic experience as they appear to have devoted their entire lives to their children, yet who passed through that phase with ease. They had exceptionally happy memories of their childhoods; one spoke of her distant, unaffectionate father but said she always felt that her mother was there only for her.

My friend, Pat, had her first baby at the same time as I did and her second a few months before mine. We lived in the same village, saw each other every day and our children were close friends from birth. Pat was a wonderful and devoted mother, immersing herself in the upbringing of her children and getting deeply involved with them on all levels. They were her babies; her emotional involvement was deep and complete.

Our elder daughters both planned to travel in the year before university. Jane left almost immediately after school finished but Pat's daughter Julie stayed in England for six months, working in a shop to save enough money for her trip. As the time drew nearer for Julie's departure, Pat got very upset. I remember her telephoning me and asking how I coped with Jane's absence. She found it hard to accept that she was not going to see Julie for five whole months and she was dreading it. Knowing Pat's investment in her family, I might have singled her out as a candidate for a fairly devastating empty nest experience. For her, though, it was a smooth transition and I asked her to write about it for me. The clue lies in the first paragraph:

I was the only child of parents in their late thirties. I had a very happy childhood with lots of loving contact with my parents, especially my mother. She always had time for me and allowed me all the usual clutter and games of early childhood.

I was married at 19 to my first real boyfriend, Paul and had my first baby in 1972 after six years of marriage. A little girl, Julie, and fortunately we 'bonded' immediately. We all enjoyed, and still do, a very close relationship, Paul and I cuddling her a great deal and me breastfeeding her until weaning age. She was always very close to us and now, aged 23, still often needs to chat over things, good and troublesome. Even when living far from home, she still needs to talk and write regularly. She is still very demonstrative with her affection. As a family, we always kiss each other hello and goodbye.

Two years after Julie, Richard was born. Another 'cuddly' baby with a very different temperament. I also bonded quickly with him and breastfed him. He was and is very self-sufficient and has always been happy in his own company. He has always also responded to open affection, though he went through a horrid aloof period when he was between 14–16. Thankfully girlfriends brought him back to normality! He is not as demonstrative as Julie but does show affection after long periods of being away.

I enjoyed the growing up years and all the many things we have shared together. I was very lucky to have been able to stay at home for those vital years, though life was quite frugal and money was scarce. Expensive outings and possessions were few and far between. The role I played over these years was one of always being there, but slowly the children were becoming more adventurous and growing in confidence. They stopped joining us on our holidays after about 15 years of age.

When Julie was 17, she announced that she wanted to take a year out after A-Levels to travel to Australia. After many different arrangements this was to be alone. When she produced the air ticket I knew she was serious. I felt then that what with the five month holiday and then university in Bradford straight afterwards, this was the moment when Julie was going to *leave home*!

I felt those last few weeks and days were slipping by and were to be treasured. We even used to say during the last week – 'Let's have our last Monday cuddle, Tuesday cuddle, etc.' When that day in April finally came I was brave, but after she went through the departure lounge door I cried and did not stop until I reached home again. I got it out of my system and convinced myself that we had turned another page in Julie's life. She was now independent and had LEFT HOME.

My life was then divided between Paul, Richard, a job and

home and my other outside interests. All these filled my days and provided I had contact with her through letters and odd calls I was quite happy. She was so excited all the time that it made me contented that she was doing what she really wanted to. However, I also shared in her 'downs' too – especially on returning from the trip and trying to settle in cold, unfamiliar Bradford. These 'Tender Loving Care' times often left me drained and her with her batteries recharged! ‐

Richard left home to go straight to university with no time out, as it were. I felt life *was* very quiet after he left because, as with Julie, he and his friends often filled the kitchen or dining room with music, chatter, dirty mugs and the smell of food cooking at odd times. I knew though that the time was right for him to move on and he thankfully fitted in very well with life at university and I could see he was happy there.

I quickly found there were lots of things to do – working full time with house and garden to see to, but most of all, Paul and I were enjoying our own company. We often see friends and in general have a very good life. I thoroughly look forward to either half term visits or other holidays and love to see all their friends descend on us at those times. But, I am always quite happy to slot back into the quieter life at the beginning of each new term. Paul and I enjoy many weekends away and both still enjoy our jobs too – we are very fortunate, especially in these difficult times.

In no way do I feel a longing for yesteryear – those days were good but life moves on. During the years of bringing up the children I had more of the daily contact with them than did Paul. I'm sure this is so with many families where Dad is out long hours at work. However, with Julie and Richard, now 23 and 21, I feel we are as close a family as we ever were. I do not feel I have suffered from 'empty nest syndrome' at all, though a day never passes without me thinking of Julie and Richard and what they are doing.

Pat is very aware of her strong, inner resources and feels they do come from the happy and secure childhood she remembers so well. Her account illustrates clearly what Ruth and Tirril have said; her sense of existence is not dependent on others and her identity and her self are intact, enabling her to move painlessly from one life stage to the next.

Maternal Feelings – Myth or Fact?

Were there other factors? Were there different strengths or degrees of maternal feeling which could cause the loss of active mothering to be more painful for some women than for others? I put this to Ruth:

> There is a mix of male and female in every individual so maternal feelings do vary. Every human being is a different mix. This is why some women have no desire at all to be mothers, some do it and don't really take to it, whereas some find it comes completely naturally. It is more difficult for those women who are almost all female, and less commonly, very largely masculine, for they have to search hard to find the other piece of themselves.

I was reminded at this point in our conversation of Miriam Stoppard's famous personal television interview with Margaret Thatcher, who has developed her masculine side almost to the total exclusion of her femaleness. Mrs Thatcher was recounting the day her twins were born and described how, when she saw them, she realized how easy it would be to be pulled in that direction, that of motherhood. The emerging of her female potential obviously alarmed her, for as she told Miriam Stoppard proudly she deflected it by applying there and then for her Bar exams, right from her hospital bed on the day she gave birth. As a friend of mine wryly remarked at the time: 'She was terrified she might turn into a woman, so she had to do something about it.' It would appear that Margaret Thatcher's highly developed animus, or masculine principle, blinded her to the fact that full-time motherhood might be a choice. Similarly, for those women who have a highly developed sense of their femaleness and whose maternal feelings are strong and immediate, the prospect of having to leave their children to return to work fills them with despair.

Ruth explained further:

> It is far easier for the women who are not immersed in this very powerful femaleness to detach more easily at the stage when children leave home. What is important about the part of us that is female is that it is about creating, and not just creating children. There are other ways to use this female creativity and this is what is so important at this stage. When you are identified with your creation, it has a life of its own, it's separate. Creativity can be channelled in many directions, into many outlets. But there are no norms where these feelings are concerned. There is no place for having a sense of cleverness at having got it right, having been 'good' at letting your children go, nor for feeling a failure if you grieve. The important thing is to want to move on.

Psychologists and therapists who use the archetypes of Greek mythology to represent different facets of human nature liken the very maternal woman to Demeter, goddess of the corn and of all growing things. This Greek myth concerns Demeter's daughter, Persephone, who is abducted by Pluto, King of the Underworld. As Persephone is out picking flowers, the ground opens under her feet and Pluto surges up through the earth in his chariot and takes Persephone down to Hades, the Kingdom of the dead. Demeter searches for her daughter in vain and goes into a terrible mourning, unable to eat or sleep, wandering the land without rest. Eventually she discovers where her daughter is, and Pluto agrees to release Persephone, though first he gives her a pomegranate from which she eats some seeds. Because she has eaten of the fruit of knowledge (echoes of the creation myth) she must spend a third of every year in the Underworld. During that time, Demeter retreats into herself and mourns; she renders the earth barren and when Persephone returns for her time on earth again, Demeter allows the crops to grow and everything flourishes once more. In *The Wise Woman* by Judy Hall and Dr Robert Jacobs, the authors acknowledge the Demeter woman:

> Demeter is the archetypal mother and nurturer: she is the

maternal instinct personified and it is the Demeter archetype who suffers from the empty nest syndrome simply because her instinct to have children is so strong and her grief at the loss of her fertility so overwhelming . . . When the Demeter woman's child leaves home she may well fall into deep depression and see this as the end, no matter what other responsibilities she may have. Her response to loss or threat is to withold nurturing: to refuse to meet the needs of others or of herself. So the Demeter woman's reaction to mid-life may well be to withdraw, to be unavailable. For instance, her children who have made lives for themselves may find that they are approved of only if that life fits into what mother knows will be right for them. Her husband may find that he has lost his wife while she struggles to let go of her children or her desire to have children. Demeter women often see themselves as victims; they give until literally they have nothing left to give and then deeply resent the calls made on their exhausted energies. Above all else, Demeter needs to learn how to say 'no', to make choices rather than to be compelled to nurture.

This sounds a bit tough on a goddess whose grief at her daughter being snatched by the King of the Underworld seems entirely understandable. But in symbolic terms we are to understand that this was Persephone's rite of passage, her leaving home, her separation from mother. Demeter was the clinging mother who withheld the harvest until her daughter returned. On the other hand, when Persephone did come back, Demeter gave the Greeks the Eleusinian mysteries, which formed the basis of Greek religion for 2000 years until the advent of Christianity. The nature of these mysteries was never revealed, though it is believed that the central theme was that of renewal and rebirth.

Perhaps the myth can help women suffering from their empty nests to understand that this is not the end; that what appears to be the closing of one stage of life signals the beginning of another. For the woman who is able to accept that her phase of active mothering has ended, that her maternal instinct is still needed but will be redirected, Hall and Jacobs give us an affirmative and hopeful Demeter woman:

The positive Demeter woman, on the other hand, has faced loss and come through with increased wisdom so she can accompany others on their journey. She has learned how to mother herself, to be her own child, with love and generosity, but also with a protective awareness that allows her to know when enough is enough (both for herself and others). She has an attunement to the cycles of nature; she understands the need for death, how to be in the dark place where new seeds sprout without constantly poking around to be sure they have germinated. She is content to wait for everything to mature in its season, knowing that the harvest will come.

Investment

The empty nest can also hit hard for those women who have invested the major part of themselves in their roles as mothers. This is not necessarily related to time spent at home, nor even to the type of mothering; rather, it concerns the emotional input to the mother role, whether this is undertaken consciously or unconsciously. When a woman allows her entire self to be absorbed by her children, when little else in her world has any real meaning for her, she is going to suffer considerable devastation when the identity which has so consumed her comes to an end. The amount of her investment will leave her bankrupt and with no other assets to call upon. As Ruth put it:

The thing you want to do most is the source of the sense of who you are. This applies whether we are talking about having a career or being a mother. A woman can be affirmed through her work or through motherhood.

Claire had heard I was writing this book and she wrote asking if she could come and talk to me about her own situation. She explained that she was just beginning to build a new life for herself and that talking about it would be part of her therapy. She also hopes that her experience will be of comfort and encouragement to other women who may feel they are in the same position. This is her story:

I always knew I wanted kids. When I was little, playing with my dolls seemed to be very real – they were my babies and I used to wonder what it would be like to be grown-up and to have real babies. I was fascinated by prams and would get my mother to lift me up to look into them. When I got a bit older, about 10 I suppose, I always had a crowd of little kids round me. I was happier with them than with children my own age. I seemed to know quite naturally how to relate to them and even at that age I can remember having strong maternal feelings and would cuddle them if they were upset or if they fell and hurt themselves.

Around about 13 I started getting those teenage magazines like *Valentine* and *Romeo*. I don't think they exist now – they were all about teen romances, very innocent. All of us girls at school had them and used to long for the day when we'd meet some tall dark handsome man! I was no different – except that I never heard the others talking about having children, except when they said things like they'd have a nice house and two children, that sort of thing. It went deeper than that for me. I didn't really think of a career, I just longed for the home and kids.

My school was highly academic and I went to university and read Maths. I had some idea that I would go on to teach but really I saw university as a hunting ground for a man – a life partner, the father of my children. I was lucky. I met Keith in my final year and we got married shortly after our graduation. I did a teaching diploma but my heart wasn't in it and I got pregnant towards the end of that year. I was ecstatic. I felt this had never happened to anyone before, I felt so incredibly important and special. I read every book there was on pregnancy, childbirth and child-rearing and went to several different antenatal classes, just so I didn't miss anything! I couldn't understand how so many women seemed to treat pregnancy as if it was something ordinary, or even something that was a nuisance. I didn't care how sick I was, how uncomfortable, it was all so worth it. This was the most important thing that had ever happened to me and there was no way that was going to be minimized.

I was very introverted during pregnancy. I stopped taking an interest in the outside world, I only thought of the baby and what it would be like when he was born. I was convinced it was a boy. Before my pregnancy I had done a great deal of reading – I was always a bit conscious that being a mathematician had left a gap in my literary education, but now I just knitted, something I wouldn't have dreamed of doing before.

Simon was born by Caesarean section and I was very disappointed at missing out on the experience of giving birth. It didn't matter though, as soon as I saw him I just fell in love. It was as simple as that. I had some early problems breast-feeding and to make matters worse Keith was jealous of the baby, but I was determined that Simon wouldn't suffer in any way. Life for my baby had to be perfect. When he was three months old, my mother suggested that she had him one afternoon a week so that I could go shopping, have some freedom to do – what? There was nothing I wanted to do that didn't include Simon. So I said no. I didn't realize at the time that it would have been rather nice for her to spend a little time with him – he was her first grandchild, after all.

When he was about one-and-a-half I discovered I was pregnant again. They found I was expecting twins and I was thrilled. Unfortunately, being a twin pregnancy and with my history, it was another Caesarean birth but it didn't matter. I had two girls, Rose and Emily. I felt I was luckier than I deserved to be. Keith took to the twins much more than he had to Simon and our earlier problems seemed to have resolved themselves.

Simon went to nursery school when he was three and I hated it. I missed him so much. I felt that someone else had taken him over and though I knew it was irrational I started to feel sad that he was growing up. I took lots of photographs of him – I wanted somehow to preserve him. When he went to school and the girls went to nursery I was inconsolable. I begged Keith to let me have another baby and though he was reluctant he eventually gave in. That was Charlotte. I used to take the three others to school with her in her pram and dreaded the day that it would be her I was leaving there. We couldn't have any more children; finances were just too tight, though I used to hope for an accident. I got very depressed when Charlotte went to school, I felt that an important part of my life had ended. Keith and my mother suggested I started teaching. I could after all, fit it in with the children's school hours but I didn't want to. I had to in the end, for money reasons and I hated the fact that I got home later than the children. I wanted to be there for them, to hear about their day at school.

I didn't really get involved with the people at my school, though I made a few friends in the staffroom. I felt I was getting a bit cabbagey – being a maths teacher doesn't give you a lot to talk abut academically and I hadn't gone back to reading. All my time, energy and thoughts seemed to be taken up with my children. My mother really shocked me one day. She said that I had become dull, that I only ever talked about the children and that I was in danger of becoming a narrow-minded obsessive mother. I remember looking at her and thinking 'You're a fine one to talk, you don't know the meaning of the word mothering'.

As the children grew older I became more and more involved with their lives which became full and very diverse. The four of them were very different and they had an enormous variety of activities and interests. I loved it all and I felt that I was the pivot around which their world revolved. They were certainly the centre of mine. I didn't mind how much ferrying around in the car I did, how much sewing of costumes for plays, how many hours spent listening to music practice or helping with homework. I felt totally stimulated by it all. I didn't have much of a social life but I didn't miss one either – my children were my companions and friends and very good company. Keith was much more detached but we were a very close family. I don't think a day passed when I didn't give thanks for having my family. They were all I had ever wanted – and more.

Of course, they grew up. They became independent. They stopped needing me in the same way. They were out for long hours and being with their friends was more important than being with the family. I still had a role, though – cooking huge meals for gangs of young people who were perpetually starving! The house was always full and I didn't dare think of what it would be like when it was empty.

I reacted badly when Simon went to university. I'm afraid I clung to him and cried when we dropped him at his hall of residence. He didn't really stay in touch very much. He made friends quickly and a gang of them took to staying in Manchester over the holidays, they all had jobs there. I felt as though some kind of bond had been cut and the pain was almost physical. I did, in fact, get excruciating abdominal pains which were investigated, but nothing was medically wrong. Then Rose and Emily left home together. They both went abroad and then Rose went to university and Emily went to train as a nurse in London. I felt as though the world I knew and felt safe in had fallen apart. I didn't seem to know who I was any longer, what my role in life was, even what the point of life was. I felt guilty because I had my four wonderful children, and in fact still had Charlotte at home but she would be gone soon and I could not see what kind of a future there would be for me. I hated my job, it seemed so pointless, so unproductive and unrewarding.

I got very depressed, lost weight, couldn't sleep, couldn't really function and had to have some time off sick. My doctor gave me anti-depressants which helped a bit but the underlying sadness was still there. I managed to get back to work, but it was as though I was doing everything through a haze. I lost all interest in sex, and that led to problems in our marriage. I tried not to cling to Charlotte but I'm afraid I didn't succeed and she reacted by becoming very distant and only being at home when it was absolutely necessary. I tried to explain to her how I felt, but that was a mistake; she was too young, and besides it wasn't fair to saddle her with my emotional deficiencies. I had heard of empty nest syndrome, but I had never known anyone to be affected as I was and I felt there was something very wrong with me. My mother was no support, in fact she was pretty scathing, but we've never been close. The strange thing was, that for the first time I was conscious of needing her to mother me, to comfort me in some way and I knew that it wouldn't happen. The depression made me feel like a child.

One day I was in the surgery having a routine blood test when I just burst into tears. The surgery nurse was very sympathetic and I just told her how I'd been feeling – it all poured out. It had been pent up, there had been no one else I could share it with and it was like a dam bursting. She arranged for me to see the counsellor attached to the practice. I have been seeing her every week and although it's painful, I'm coming to understand a great deal about myself and my relationship with my children.

I had a lonely, unhappy childhood myself, with a cold, unaffectionate mother (I was unplanned and unwanted when I arrived). I know that I longed for that affection and I found it first of all in my dolls, who were very real to me, and then in the children I used to 'mother' when only a child myself. I know that it filled a cold, empty hole in me. The counsellor has helped me to see that my longing for children and my feelings about them when I had them were an unconscious attempt to create the warmth and love I had not had earlier. It was like having a second chance.

I think it will be a long haul but I am beginning to believe, though very tentatively, that I will find an identity for myself that is not just 'mother' and that there will be life beyond children. And of course, I haven't lost them. They will always be my children. I just have to learn how to separate from them. What I did, from the moment I was first pregnant, was to put all my emotional eggs in one basket.

Liz is a schoolteacher with two sons; the elder is 25 and has been through university. Her younger son was about to start when she wrote to me. She described how hard it had been when her elder son had left home and how she had worked during the intervening six years to change her attitude:

I realize now that my deep sense of loss when my son left stemmed from the way I had constructed my relationship with him, based on elements of control and dependence: I very much depended on my children to provide my sense of identity which affected my sense of well-being and happiness.

Unwittingly I encouraged their dependence on me, not realizing my growing dependence on them. To 'let go' of my influence over them meant that I felt diminished, and my sense of identity was eroded. I can see now that it was essential for the development of my older son that he got away and that the umbilical cord was finally cut.

How I came to revise my approach to mothering is hard to document. The most important step I took was to return to education for myself, starting with an assertiveness course in Applied Psychology, and then a Master's degree in education which I completed last year.

I chose the courses initially because I was depressed: I felt a lack of direction, little sense of identity and had little self-esteem. I had attempted over the years to become the 'perfect mother' and had invested a lot of myself in this process. When my sons reached adolescent years they began to challenge my role. I found this very hard to cope with as it undermined my position.

The reading and thinking which have been part of these courses have helped me to look at my relationships and in some ways to recognize them. There are two vital areas I rethought which have relevance here. One thing that I had to come to terms with was that I do not 'own' my children. I needed to move away from the position of ownership and control. I gradually came to understand the importance of my support for my sons as they take responsibility for themselves, that neither of us is dependent on the other, but that we try to foster a sense of respect and interdependency within the family.

What was also very exciting to discover was that developing potential does not depend on age and that at 59 I can embark on another venture which involves new learning and different skills, at the same time as my son goes to university to develop his potential.

What is important is that I do not see the enormous steps that he is taking as 'leaving', or worse still as 'rejecting' me, but that it is part of our growing and living, to be faced with optimism.

There are other, discernible reasons for a particularly painful empty nest experience. As Tirril Harris points out, for some women it is very often not the children's leaving home that causes pain but the feeling that they are no longer valued as mothers:

> The actual leaving home of the children feels less important if the mothering role is still valued and if the woman knows this. Her role and identity is still intact; she is still a mother even when they have left. If that role feels as though it has been taken away, then sadness and grief result.

This is far from uncommon; when young people leave home, they often make a bid for autonomy and independence. It is nearly always a temporary transitional stage, lasting while they prove to themselves and to us that they can live without our help, thereby 'cutting the apron strings'. But this can feel like rejection to the mother who only weeks before may have been fully involved in helping with A-Level revision, giving support during exams, accompanying her children on university visits, helping to plan a wedding, furnishing a new flat or searching 'situations vacant' columns with anxious offspring. This aloof phase is usually temporary (see Chapter Six) but is painful while it lasts.

Self-esteem

An important determining factor in the development of severe empty nest syndrome, and one that is usually tied up with all of the above causes, is low self-esteem. The woman who cannot recognize her intrinsic worth may obtain a vicarious sense of value through her children. The woman with poor self-esteem may be emotionally fed by the unconditional approval of her very young children, this then, can shape her idea of who she is and what she does well. She may then invest a great deal in her children's achievements, even, perhaps, becoming a pushy parent so that their success becomes her glory. Or she may become the 'perfect' mother, experiencing pride in her children's beautifully washed and ironed clothes, their home-cooked meals served on time, their nice manners, their obedience. Her children become the template on which she patterns herself and as long as they are there for her she has a source of pride, and again, a very definite role.

And then they are gone and she is lost, bereft, drifting. She looks inside herself and finds nobody at home; the person she sees herself to be is miles away at university with her son, in her new job with her daughter. And she collapses, deflated, like a pricked balloon and often sinks into a deep depression.

Single Parents

I do not want to be too categorical about this, as, with most things, there are variables. It is not a question of single mothers automatically feeling more bereft than their married counterparts; many married women have expressed a sense of isolation compounded by their husband's lack of understanding or impatience surrounding their wives' feelings of loss and bereavement. However, the woman who has brought up her children on her own for most or all of their lives is more vulnerable to feelings of deep loss than the woman who has a happy, stimulating relationship with a husband or partner. For the single mother the children are her primary relationship, she sees them grow up in her image, shaped by her influences. As they grow up they become a source of friendship and bonds tend to knit very closely. When the children of a single mother leave home, she really is on her own and often the empty nest highlights the desolation of her single state.

This tends to be particularly marked in single mothers with one child. They become in effect, partners, especially as the child grows up and adult activities and decisions are shared – and without being sexist, the sense of partnership is even stronger if that child is a son. The relationship between a single mother and her son can be intensely close, and though for this reason it is desirable that the son should leave home as soon as possible after school finishes, for the mother it is like losing both child and partner.

Cara was married at 22 and the following year she had a son, Gabriel. Two years later, her husband left her, saying that he felt too young to be tied down to marriage and fatherhood. He visited Gabriel for about a year but then drifted out of their lives. Cara was determined that her son should suffer as little as possible; she put all her energies into being mother and father to Gabriel:

Times were hard. John (her ex-husband) occasionally sent a sum of money for Gabriel but didn't pay any regular maintenance, nor did the authorities manage to pin him down. There was no Child Support Agency in those days. So I had to go out to work. I hated leaving my little boy but I had no option. I wasn't qualified for anything but I got a clerk's job in an office. It didn't pay much, but it kept us together. My mother had Gabriel when I was at work, as fortunately we lived in the same town, but when he was six she died. After that it was childminders after school but nothing was very consistent – either they moved, or gave up and I had to find someone else. I was worried about the lack of continuity, though Gabriel was very happy at school.

I felt it was absolutely vital that the time I spent with him should be really meaningful – what the Americans call 'quality time' – so that even without a father figure in his life, I could somehow give him a foundation that would stand him in good stead. I was always there for him at bedtime when he was small, and we always had a meal together when I got home from work. There were men in my life, but I never let anything become serious. For one thing, I didn't want to be out a lot in the evenings, nor did I want Gabriel to have a series of 'uncles' passing through the house, and particularly not in my bed. If I had met someone I wanted to live with or marry, that would have been different, but I didn't. That part was lonely, I must admit, because after all, I was still pretty young, but I felt there would be time for all that when Gabriel no longer needed me.

I enjoyed his teenage years. Although I was anxious about the lack of a father, he had a good role model in my brother, to whom I am very close, and I felt that Tom took care of that side of things as well as anyone who wasn't a father could do. When he was 15, I went to college to study for a degree, part-time – I felt I wanted something stimulating for when he left home. I enjoyed the fact that we were both studying at the same time and I felt that I was using my brain at last.

Those were particularly good years. The house was always full of his friends, there was noise and laughter and conversation and music and great vitality surging through the place. I was fascinated watching him become a man. He became very protective towards me – a reversal of roles. He was thoughtful, doing things like getting in the coal, taking out the dustbins, all sorts of things like that without being asked. He became the man of the house and seemed to enjoy the responsibility. He made me install a burglar alarm because he was so concerned at the spate of burglaries we had had in the area. But it wasn't just all the practical things. By the time he was 18, I found I was relying on him quite a lot emotionally. The relationship between us was so close, so marvellous. There was something about it that was almost an equality, as though we were two adults, not mother and son. Don't get me wrong, though. I love being his mother.

He wanted to be a doctor and went to university to read Medicine when he was 19 after doing a third A-Level year. He talked it all through with me at every stage, showing me university prospectuses, asking my advice. I went to look round the places with him when he went for interviews and felt part of it all, and very thrilled about what he was doing.

Then suddenly it seemed it was October. He packed up his room, I drove him to the university and helped him settle in his hall of residence and drove home with tears almost blinding me. I cannot describe how I felt. I was devastated. I felt as though I had been bereaved and I felt more lonely that I could ever have believed possible.

Gabriel was good at keeping in touch at first. He didn't write but he'd ring and ask how things were and say 'Are you doing alright, Mum?' I hadn't said anything, but he was aware of how much I missed him. I tried to be cheerful and tell him my bits of news, though they sounded trivial compared with the exciting work he was doing. I was still doing my degree but I even thought of dropping it and training as a nurse so I'd have

something in common with him. His phone calls got less
frequent. I knew he was having a good time and that he needed
to break away from me. I was pleased in one part of me that I'd
made a success of bringing him up alone, but I felt as though
someone had taken away part of my body.

As the months went by, it got worse, not better. I became
very depressed and felt that my son was now out of reach. It
seemed as though he had been the whole purpose of my
existence – I had him when I was quite young, so he'd been
there for nearly all my adult life. I had given myself completely
to him and now I felt totally empty. I gave up my degree
because I couldn't concentrate on my studies. I couldn't eat
and lost a lot of weight. I couldn't talk to my friends about
how I felt because they were all so pleased that Gabriel was
doing so well, and they congratulated me on doing a good job.
If only you knew, I thought.

Eventually I went to my doctor. He offered me anti-
depressants and a chance to have counselling at a local day
centre with a community psychiatric nurse. I agreed to the
counselling but not to the tablets. I wasn't against them in
principle, but I felt they might mask the real feelings that I
knew I had to deal with. The counselling has been excellent.
I've been seeing the nurse once a week for three months now
and she has helped me to see that Gabriel had become more
than just my son – he had taken the place, in my mind, of my
husband, or of any other partner I might have had and in a way,
I had developed an emotionally incestuous relationship with
him. That sounds strong, but it's the only way really to
describe it. The nurse has also helped me to appreciate that my
main purpose with Gabriel was to bring him up to be strong
and independent and whole and that I succeeded in that and
that I must not lose sight of what an achievement it is. I am still
feeling low, but not half as bad as I was. I think it is probably
fairly common for this to happen with single parents, especially
if there is only one child. After all, you do become a
partnership, a twosome. The nurse explained how sometimes
this can grow into a mutually dependent relationship where the
child cannot break away and often stays at home well into

adulthood, not fulfilling any of his or her potential and remaining emotionally crippled. That makes me shudder. One day, perhaps, I will have grandchildren and I can look forward to that. Meanwhile, mother and son are both doing well!

What About The Men?

It is interesting that though many of the women I have spoken to or who have written to me have had a good deal to say about the changing relationship with their husbands, very little mention has been made of the father's feelings when his child leaves home. What seems to occur most frequently is that the woman feels grief, sadness, loneliness, redundancy, while her partner does not know how to cope with her emotions. Some are dismissive and openly unsympathetic, while some make a great effort to understand their wives' despair, but feel impotent and rather bewildered. 'He/She has not died, only left home' is a typical male remark, repeated many times in the accounts I received. This would certainly suggest that this is not on the whole a great difficulty for fathers, though certainly some *are* affected.

Graham Taylor, former England football manager was one such father; the day he left his 18-year-old daughter at college, he said, was one of the worst of his life: 'I have never felt so empty, lonely and upset as the day she started her own life'. One friend said that her husband hardly reacted when their two sons left home, but that on the day their only daughter left for university, he wept openly and was inconsolable for some weeks.

There may be a clue in the reactions of these two men. Our culture does not encourage men to become emotionally close to their sons. The majority of fathers and sons still find it difficult to show physical affection, such as hugging and kissing, just as men are not demonstrative with their friends. But the closeness between fathers and daughters is recognized and therefore allowed. The idea of a daughter, even a grown-up daughter being 'daddy's little girl' is a culturally familiar one. To a certain extent, then, fathers can allow themselves to show a degree of regret that their daughters have grown up, left home and become independent – and of course, possibly 'replaced' their fathers with a partner.

Some close questioning among friends who are fathers produced interesting results. When asked how they felt about their children leaving home, the consensus was that they were pleased to see them taking their place in the world, they were proud of their achievements, and they enjoyed it when they came back home for a visit. Yes, I said, that is fine, but how do you *feel*? This question caused a modicum of discomfort at first, given the male resistance to talking about feelings (*pace* all the exceptions to this – I know you exist.) Gradually, though, some of these men dipped their toes in the water of their unexamined emotions:

> I often think back to when they were little and realize how much I enjoyed them then. I knew what their needs were, what my role was and how to provide for them. Now they seem so independent and self-sufficient – if they have anything they want to discuss, they tend to do it with my wife. I feel a bit redundant.

> Now that my son has left home, I wish I had developed a closer relationship with him. He was at boarding school and I feel I never really got to know him. I always thought it would occur naturally when he grew up because then we would be men together, but he is very different from me and I would like to understand him better. I'm not sure how to get close to him now he's gone, and hope that perhaps when he is older we will find we've got some sort of shared ground.

> I don't actually miss them but I wish they were still here. What I mean is that I am so immersed in work that I don't have time or space to think about missing them, but if I do think about the fact that they've gone I feel nostalgic and would like to turn the clock back. But it doesn't upset me. They are doing what they want to do and I feel I've played a part in that.

The other men I talked to maintained a fairly cerebral response to the matter of their children leaving home. Some said that they had never been involved in the intimate, day-to-day business of bringing up children and that their relationship was perhaps a more objective one. Undoubtedly fathers miss their children, some more than others, but their biological and emotional ties are different. This is a good thing for it creates a balance. The only problem arises through the man's inability to understand or tolerate his wife's sadness, though many try to be supportive. I cannot draw definite conclusions, for I have not thoroughly researched this area, but I think it is reasonable to suggest that men do not usually suffer greatly from empty nest syndrome.

What can and often does happen is that the children's departure acts as a catalyst in the relationship between their parents. The years of concentrated effort which go into bringing up children, advancing a career and staying financially afloat can be all-consuming, relegating the relationship between partners to an exhausted backwater. Some couples find that without the common bond of children they no longer have anything to say to each other when the children have gone; both have changed over the years and so they find they are waking up with a stranger. When this happens, the marriage may end or it may continue out of habit, or the couple may recognize what has happened and work at finding each other again.

Happily, many couples find renewed vigour in their relationship and enjoy the opportunity to have the house to themselves, to do things again as a couple and to share in the pleasure and sense of achievement of having done the job of parenting well. These couples are fortunate, for it does seem that where the relationship is alive and vital, a woman's empty nest sadness diminishes more quickly as she readjusts to her role as half of a couple. Some of the research carried out on families in later life does suggest that marital happiness is high during the empty nest period, with partners taking a renewed interest in each other's personalities and hobbies.

I was interested in the response to a magazine article I wrote on empty nest syndrome. The magazine titled it *Falling in Love Again* and illustrated it with a picture of two dreamy eyed, young, impossibly good looking, supposedly middle-aged parents! Some women wrote to me and said how true, they did feel as though they had fallen in love (with their husbands) again, while others were quite angry or cynical at such an idea (I felt like writing back and saying I hadn't given the article its title!)

What is Normal?

While writing this book, I have often been asked what constitutes a 'normal' degree of empty nest syndrome. This is an important question, though not one with an easy, definitive answer. Many women experience very deep feelings of loss akin to bereavement which may last for several months or longer, yet they do not become clinically depressed, as Cara did, and they do come through it. It is perhaps a little like wondering when to send for the doctor if someone has a chest infection; it may be relatively benign and clear up, it may need a course of antibiotics or it may turn to pneumonia. Unlike a chest infection, though, women suffering when their children have left home are likely to hide it. It is difficult to ascertain when feelings move from normal grieving to a pathological condition requiring treatment (the checklist for depression on *page 119* is a good guide).

In 1993, a shocked nation learned of the death of Nicolette Powell, wife of singer Georgie Fame, who committed suicide by jumping off Bristol's famous Clifton Suspension Bridge. The life of the couple, who had married after Nicolette's divorce from the Marquess of Londonderry, was 'idyllic, until the children grew up'. The inquest heard how she had slumped into depression after her four children left home, feeling that there was no point or purpose in her life. She made a first suicide attempt in 1992, taking a massive overdose of drugs and alcohol. Although she survived, and for a time seemed to get better, her depression returned.

While this is obviously an extreme case, and one in which Nicolette Powell's depression was almost certainly compounded by other factors, it is a sober reminder that women who are already vulnerable to depression sometimes do report feeling suicidal when their children have left home. Dr Robert Bor, of City University, London has stated that:

Apart from birth and death, a child leaving home is the most far-reaching transition any family deals with. It should be recognized as a very stressful period – it's very common.

What we need is more openness about the empty nest syndrome, more acceptance of its existence and of the pain and loneliness it can cause. Women need a support network which includes friends, family and health professionals, who are able to recognize that this is a stressful time, and not minimize or dismiss the implications. If consciousness can be raised in general, women who are particularly vulnerable can be helped to understand the possible reasons for their acutely distressing reactions and much could then be done to alleviate the isolation, grief, depression and hopelessness that these women experience.

4 NEVER THE SAME AGAIN: CHANGE, LOSS AND IDENTITY

*She said how terrible she felt when all hers had left home.
How she'd gone to the library and looked for a book
about grief that described how you could feel real grief
when this happened. Only they hadn't got a book like
that, she said, only books about grief through death.*
From Marriage Guidance *a short story by Susan Davis*

The feelings of loss when children leave home can be devastating
in their intensity. The void, the pain and the grief are all often overwhelming, and closely akin to bereavement. Many of the hallmarks
of bereavement are present – a woman may pace the house, find it
difficult to go into that child's bedroom – and weep uncontrol-
lably. Yet she has not been bereaved and this compounds the situation by introducing feelings of guilt. There is no recognized rite of
passage for the time when children leave home, so the grieving
mother's feelings are not acknowledged by society. She is likely to
come up against a wall of incomprehension if she tries to talk about
her pain. After all, there is no body. Her child is alive and well and
doing what children do when they grow up – in fact their
successful leaving to build a life for themselves is the proof that we
have done our job well, and though we can and should take
comfort from that, it is difficult to rationalize when you feel so raw.

The power of these emotions can be demonstrated by the way
they affect even those women who do not expect to feel that way,
like Alison, whose thinking is entirely positive, who believe, as she
did, that crossing this threshold is a smooth and natural part of
motherhood:

I could never understand these women who seemed to mope about when their children left home. After all, that's what our job is all about – to bring them up to fly the nest. Both mine went to university and I was so proud of them. Friends asked if I missed them and I didn't think about that, I was too keen to boast about them – after all, they had both got into Oxford! But after the last one went, I found I was getting very depressed. I had no idea why, I felt low all the time and actually physically unwell. I went to the doctor and she cottoned on straightaway. 'You're mourning for the loss of your children' she told me and as soon as she said it, I realized she was right.

The extent and depth of these feelings may be recognized as very real by someone else who can provide support, like Alison's doctor, but on the whole a sense of isolation is an inseparable part of the loss. Husbands and partners often find it difficult to provide support; either they are coping with their own feelings of loss or they do not understand the woman's intense grief and they become impatient. So the woman feels alone with her pain.

My daughter left home two years ago to pursue a college course in Southampton and the only word I can find to describe my feelings is bereavement. I miss her dreadfully but I keep my tears to myself. I don't really think people want to know about this.

Why does it feel like bereavement? They are independent and I smile and encourage them because I know it's right to do so. I sit on her bed and cannot stop crying. I really wonder if it is possible to die of a broken heart. I know that sounds melodramatic but I feel so alone. It reassured me when Denise Robertson, the agony aunt, said on television that she felt like that when it happened to her, but no one I know shares this pain. Most of my contemporaries cannot identify with it and seem blasé about their children leaving home. This makes me feel like an alien – or at least a very unhinged and emotionally unstable person. I don't believe that this pain will ever heal itself. I only hope that I will learn to adjust to it.

I am writing this with tears pouring down my face. I am in danger of of alienating my husband, family and good friends – and why? Because my son has gone off to university. I am driving everyone crazy with my despondency and nothing they say can cheer me up or make me snap out of it. I feel a physical pain and a sense of loss similar to a bereavement, something my husband keeps pointing out, 'You carry on as if he's dead', he keeps telling me. The strange thing is that I have friends whose children have gone away to university or abroad this summer and yet they do not seem to feel the way I do. Some are even pleased and this is totally beyond me.

We moved when the children were 18 and 19 and they decided to stay in their home town. I can't describe how bereft I felt. I know you've got to let them go, that they've got to live their own lives, but it felt terrible. I've got their photos all over the house and every time I saw them I just burst into tears. My husband said 'I just don't know what to do'. You miss the silly little things. I even miss tidying up after them. Things just aren't the same.

We spend their childhoods teaching them to learn to do things for themselves – everything from tying their shoelaces to applying for jobs and then when they grow up the relationships change, they become your friends and it's just at that stage that they say 'bye-bye' and that is part of the great sadness.

It is clear from the number of women who have written and spoken to me that this experience is far from uncommon yet time and again the feeling of being the only one, of not having friends who also felt this way, was expressed, increasing the pain of isolation. The very fact that there are so many women with these powerful feelings of grief suggests that it is much more common than is realized. The truth, I believe, is that for every woman who is afraid to let her feelings be known there is at least one counterpart, apparently coping, apparently accepting the emptiness of the empty nest. It is sad that we cannot share this at a time when the friendship and sisterhood of other women is particularly important, and sad, too, that so many feel the need to conceal their vulnerability in order to prove that they have 'got it right', that their children really are happy and independent and that to weep for their absence would be not only foolish but somehow unnatural. So primed are we to be good mothers in this way that not only are we often ashamed to admit to these intense feelings, we can even deceive ourselves.

Lynne wrote to me after a conversation we had about the emotions that accompany this period in a woman's life:

> I was shocked that you talked about women feeling as though they had been bereaved when their children left home. This is a perfectly natural development in the process of mothering and we should be proud, not sad, to see our offspring making new lives for themselves. My feelings about my sons leaving home are entirely positive – in no way does it diminish me.

Fair enough – though I thought Lynne's use of the word 'shocked' was rather revealing. It seemed to me an overreaction to what is a reality for so many. More was revealed, though, later on in her letter, when she had presumably forgotten that such feelings were unacceptable:

> When he (*her first son*) left, I felt as though part of me had died and would never again come alive.

Here is a case where Lynne is responding so greatly to external conditioning that she failed to recognize her own grief. Yet it is perfectly valid to feel like this. It is a reaction to loss, to change and to uncertainty, and for many women, to the feeling that their world has been turned upside down or even obliterated completely.

How could this not be about loss? For so many women, motherhood brings a deeply primitive sense of fulfilment, wholeness, completion and identity. When we feel as though that most fundamental sense of our identity is being eroded we face not only emptiness and a sense of bereavement, but also the realization that life will never be the same again. We may find ourselves wondering who we will become and where we will go from here. Some women, especially if they are suffering from depression find themselves asking 'Is this it?', unable to see a future for themselves.

The following women's stories illustrate how profound is this combination of grief, loss and the struggle to find the way ahead.

Susan's story:

Susan's husband had undergone a long period of uncertainty and unemployment when he found a job in a county several hundred miles from their home in Oxfordshire. He moved first, living in lodgings during the week, and their daughters aged 16 and 18 were excited at the prospect of new places and people and couldn't wait for the move. But this precipitated changes; the elder daughter's boyfriend, seeing the prospect of losing her, asked her to marry him and she moved in with him.

I felt breathless and helpless, yet totally relieved that our beloved, exacting, demanding, wearing, temperamental, high-handed daughter was happy and beginning her new life. But before Caroline moved out I sobbed my heart out one evening after dinner because I didn't know the rules – could I visit, and when? Could I phone, and when? Had I done enough for her? Had I taught her enough? – she was, after all, only 18. She was very reassuring, but for me it was all too final; if she were going to college she'd be home in the holidays. She explained that she would never have gone to college, that this was right for her and at least she had a job she enjoyed. And I coped when it came to it because she was only on the other side of town.

Louisa, the younger one, was working in a newsagent's but left when we moved later that year. Why are mothers always the last to see the obvious? On the drive to our new home, this once enthusiastic daughter was lethargic, apathetic and quite miserable. She was invited back to a party the following weekend and on her return she asked if we would mind if she went back the next weekend to help out in the shop as they were desperate and it would be easier for them to have someone who knew the job. When she got back she asked if we could go for a coffee. My sixth sense was at last in working order; bells which should have rung at least three weeks ago were suddenly deafening. We sat down in a crowded café and my daughter asked if we would mind if she went back to Oxford to live as she and the shop manager couldn't live without each other. My thoughts as we sat there just swarmed round my head clamouring for attention; I felt as though someone was beating my head with metal fists as I calmly told her that if she was sure that this was right for her then that was what she must do. My stomach was churning, I felt sick, I just wanted to scream to everyone to stop! What they were doing was unimportant – this was my daughter telling me that my mothering days were over – no more joyous kitchen cookery sessions, no more two hour stints with me relaxing in the bath after teaching and her pouring out her soul about not knowing what her purpose in life was, and why she didn't believe in God; no house filled with young laughter, music, continuous TV, clothes slung across chairs, shoes strategically placed for father to trip over; no more desperate 'Can you wash this for me (at 11.30 pm) I need it first thing . . .'

I didn't cry then. When the time came, I took her to the station, the solitary passenger on the platform like a scene from Dr Zhivago. When she was out of sight I went into the town, not knowing where I was going. I meandered round the shops knowing what those poor women who shoplift due to PMT must feel like, trying to pull myself together to get home and cheer the dogs and Louisa's cat. My husband had appeared very philosophical but that night we went to bed early and crawled into each other's arms and wept together. Since then I haven't wept very much, I just feel terribly bereft at times, so empty inside. Why bake? Why keep the table tidy? I just leave enough space for two to eat and let the rest remain cluttered otherwise it's too tidy. I have woken in the night several times with a wet face and sobbed, no howled out loud, the howl coming from the depths of my birthgiving and irrationally I can't wait for my first grandchild when my mothering may come in useful again. The empty nest took a lot of building . . .

Pauline's story:

Pauline prepared herself for the separation by starting a part-time degree while her daughter was still at home. However, this did not lessen her grief which was perhaps exacerbated by the fact that she enrolled at the same college her daughter was to attend:

> I imagined I would be far too engrossed in my own studies to sit around moping. However, when the day arrived for her departure, I felt as though I had been kicked senseless, even though the college she was attending was less than an hour's drive away and the same college that I was already studying at. Everything in me hurt as we packed clothes, teddies, guitars and academic paraphernalia. I couldn't eat all that day. We drove her to her appointed digs, settled her in, hung about longer than was necessary, tried to kiss her without crying or clinging and dashed to the car. I cried all the way home. I could not go into her room for a week. I heard her voice all over the house, looked at the clock when the school bus was due and started crying all over again. I 'saw' her in the garden, on the stairs, everywhere I looked she was there. I truly felt bereaved and that I was mourning a deep loss.
>
> Sometimes I would catch sight of her at college, although we were on different courses, and whilst my heart lifted to see her so happy, it was hard to try and wave casually without dashing over to hug her or tell her to get more sleep, wear a coat or get her shoes repaired. I could not fulfil my 'mothering role' and I felt redundant and at a loss to know how to cope. My husband understood my feelings and whilst he missed her very much, he thought that my loss was more acute because my daughter and I were so close. Gradually I came to be able to go into her room but my emotions were very near the surface and it only took a scribbled message on her board or a pinned up birthday card from a friend to start me crying again. Every time she came home it was like someone had switched the light on in the house and every time she went back I felt plunged into gloom and drabness. This lasted for about 18 months and then gradually I began to be able to say goodbye without tears. I was able to visit places we had been together without thinking

'We sat here and had coffee, etc.'. I worried still all the time about her safety. I still do, her health, social life and all the other millions of things that mothers take on board.

She is now in her third year of teaching, lives with her fiancé in their own house and is still less than an hour's drive away, so I am very fortunate that we are in close contact still. However, if I go past a school at home time, I feel a real aching hurt that will bring tears to my eyes. Every time she visits and draws up outside the house, it is as though the sun has just come out from behind the clouds and I start being a mother once more. I am still vulnerable, though, and if I hope we may visit one weekend only to find that they are going out elsewhere, I begin to feel a sadness that has to be nipped in the bud by taking on a household task.

My son had already left home when my daughter came to leave, so although I had that awful experience once it did nothing to soften the blow, even though I had tried to prepare myself better for it, when the time came it was just as dreadful. I don't think I will ever get over not having her live here and still refer to her old room as Anne's room. I still keep all her old letters, cards and general childhood mementoes. I miss her every day and even writing this piece has brought all the hurt and loneliness back – mistakes may be due to tears in my eyes.

Penny's story:
Penny suffered the loss of both daughters and her husband at the same time. This sort of multiple loss is not uncommon around this time and makes the empty nest itself much harder to bear:

It happens to us all, of course, mothers, and I was no exception. The time comes for our chicks to fly the nest. What made it particularly difficult was the fact that they chose to leave within about a month of each other. My two daughters, both of whom I adore, my best friends. Amanda, my eldest, 19 years old, went to live with a young man she fell in love with when she nursed him. What can you do? Nothing that doesn't sound selfish, so you hold back your tears and your tongue.

My youngest daughter, just 17, went to live with a man 10

years older than her. I could have stopped her then, I suppose, but she would only have rebelled against me and gone anyway, so I let her go.

I never in my wildest dreams imagined that life could be so empty. When the kids are babies, you envisage what it must be like not to have the responsibility of those other lives every day, and you think of all the things you'll do when you have your own life back again, but it is not like that. All the things you always meant to do somehow just don't seem important. All you can think of is filling the endless, very quiet day, all that peace that you once longed for is no longer what you want, and time lies heavy on you.

In my own case, the month before my eldest left home I found out that my husband was having an affair. I don't blame him entirely now, though I certainly did then. Strange how your mind changes over the years. I was not then the person that I am now, and can see with hindsight the reasons for his infidelity. Too late now, of course, as the marriage is long gone. At the time I was devastated. The girls' leaving was made worse because of the isolation I felt at home. Unable to turn to my husband because of the rift between us, I felt something closely akin to the grief of bereavement, without a body. Money was not a problem then, but having money to spend induced in me no feelings of pleasure, despite the fact the money had been tight for many years. My husband, unable to comfort me in any way, used to tell me to 'go out and buy yourself a new frock', thinking in a typical male way that that was the panacea needed to stop that dreadful melancholia, experienced, I'm sure, by so many mothers.

It took me about a month, I suppose, to stop being a blubbering heap, during which time I took a long hard look at myself. I have always been low on self-esteem and I realized that my husband wasn't making my life any easier. Having to live with the constant reminder of his infidelity was too much for me, and although it was very painful at the time I asked him to leave. That was many years ago, and both mine and my daughters' lives have changed drastically since then. I never really lost them, and of course you rarely do. Amanda is living just down the road, and Sherry is living nearby too, she's a mother herself now. We've talked about that time over the years and they both know now how badly I took their leaving, though I didn't tell them at the time in case it upset them.

It's the way of the world, children have to leave home. The secret, if there is one, is to make a life for yourself while the children are still with you. It's a terrible onus to put on your children that they are the sole meaning of your life.

Rosie's story:

Rosie's husband was in the Merchant Navy and often away for long periods, during which she feels she compensated by becoming specially close to her three children:

I realized that my children would soon leave home and as this was the last chance to spend time with them I gave up my job. This meant I was able to support them through the last stages of study and during their A-Levels, and it was no great sacrifice for me as I have always been happier as a housewife/gardener/home decorator.

My elder daughter graduated in July and returned home to set about finding a job, so for several weeks I had a full house with my husband returning home every other week. In October the 'crunch' came. My 18-year-old twins, a boy and a girl, went to university and I was left absolutely desolate. I had prepared to a certain extent and we had arranged a holiday in the Dordogne for the week after the twins left, but then my husband had his leave cancelled and my elder daughter, still with no job, went away to stay with her boyfriend. I was suddenly left in a large empty house with all my plans cancelled feeling totally redundant and useless. I cried and moped around trying to keep occupied. I painted woodwork, tidied cupboards and drawers and wore myself out.

We finally had a holiday in November, in Spain, but I woke tearful every morning and became very emotional over a stray dog that followed us for eight miles or so while walking in the hills one day. On our return I was determined to pull myself together and plan for Christmas which I usually find an awful chore and a lot of unappreciated effort. Everyone would be coming home and I determined to make it the best ever. At this stage my elder daughter finally got a job. I was sad to see her go but she was restless and had not settled down again since returning home from university and her departure was quite a relief.

Christmas went really well, but seeing the twins again as they really were and not as the babies, toddlers and teenagers of my memories made me realize that they were ready to face the outside world, were well equipped to do so as I had done a good job in preparing them, and that sad as it was, life at home would never be the same again. They both phone home frequently (we provided them with BT Chargecards), my son, surprisingly, more than my daughter.

My husband and I have filled the empty space in the house and it is a real treat to be able to get into the bathroom, use the computer and choose what to record on the video machine. Although I do feel sad when I have to go into their bedrooms for any reason. We have been away for short breaks and have had friends to stay without having to move out of our bedroom and sleep on the airbed on the sitting room floor.

I have decided not to rush out and get another job, but fill my time doing all the creative things I have wanted to do and never had time for. I am taking a computer literacy course and a St John's First Aid Course. I have been on an Animal Welfare Demonstration, first demonstration ever, and have had time to write plenty of letters of protest.

And we still have our beautiful 'family' of 14 cats who create quite a lot of work and provide good company for me.

Lucy's story:
Lucy is one of many women who believed that it couldn't happen to her:

I thought the empty nest syndrome was something that happened to other people, mostly to people in the past. I had been wearing jeans for over 20 years, was a single mother with a career and interests. I was mum the chum. It would be

different. I wouldn't cling. Their leaving would just be another
phase like exchange visits to France and driving lessons, A-
Levels, UCAS forms. It hadn't occurred to me that I would
feel so bereft, that I would miss them as babies and as best
friends, all at the same time.

Elaine's story:

How can I put into words this concoction of emotions I am
experiencing? My children, aged 20 and 17 have been to
weekly boarding school since the age of eight. 'Easy' you
might say, 'You haven't had them to look after every day – so
why do you miss them so much now?' When they came home
at weekends and holidays we concentrated our efforts into
enjoying their company and the company of their friends. We
always had a houseful at weekends but now they are at
university they come home less frequently and we miss them.
We supported them in all their sporting activities, we were a
taxi service for them, had numerous 'extras' staying over at
weekends and school holidays and now it's just the two of us
and I feel redundant.

Nothing prepared me for this empty nest syndrome. There are
numerous baby books but where does one turn to for help at this
time of life – I feel as though I am treading water waiting for
something to happen. I have neglected my home, myself and my
husband and I feel totally preoccupied with my emptiness. I am
shutting out my feelings and glossing over the pain.

I have a busy life running a small farmhouse bed and
breakfast and dinner parties for paying guests but my role as
mother is changing rapidly. I know I must come to terms with
their new found freedom and independence. I don't want
them to feel guilty about my inability to handle this situation,
but I am afraid I have laid the emotional blackmail on a bit. My
husband has been super in all this and has tried to explain to
the children how I am feeling. I hope they can understand a
little and most of all, I hope they don't feel pressured into
coming home. I am trying to be positive about this new phase
in my life and recharging my batteries ready for whatever
comes next.

Selina's story:

When my 18-year-old daughter – my second child – left home
this summer to go abroad for her gap year, I was beside myself.
This had not happened with so much force when my son went
abroad and I have tried to understand why. I cast around
desperately to find something to read on the subject and found
nothing and only found solace with one particular friend, a
scientist and lecturer who, when her daughter had gone
abroad, had suffered a minor nervous breakdown.

When my daughter was two-and-a-half she was found to
have a very virulent tumour in her face and she went through
radiotherapy and 18 months of chemotherapy. It affected us all
as a family, and this binds you to a child like nothing else. My
pride in her bravery, her fighting spirit and her achievements is
immense.

I lead a very full and busy life and have always done so. But
from the time of her study leave in May until she went away
was a special time. The phone was busy, she was out a lot. We
went to San Francisco together and I felt this terrible
impending sense of loss, a bereavement – for the time that was
and will never be again, for my loss as a mother and for my
inability to protect her.

Well, she went away and settled well and is happy and that is
what has given me my strength. Though I have a constant
ache, to know that she is happy and enjoying life and is now
mature enough to cope with being away has made me able to
cope too.

The depth of feeling on this subject and the number of
women who suffer, especially for many of those experiencing
menopause, is immense. We don't want to be told to pull
ourselves together and other such trite statements.

Maureen's story:

I just couldn't believe it was happening to me. I knew about
the empty nest syndrome but as a full-time lecturer in further
education I expected to ride out the changes brought by adult
children very much as I had the problems of the menopause –
too busy to notice overmuch.

Both my children have graduated and are working abroad. My husband and I are at home, redundant parents. One part of my mind tells me that we have been very successful parents but mostly all I feel is the loneliness. My husband says very little but jumps quickly to the phone when it rings and is clearly disappointed if the caller is not one of our children.

My job, which I have always enjoyed, is now only a means of filling time until we can manage a visit to them or they to us. I feel that my life has come to an end. A very dramatic statement, I know, but I think this is the only way to convey the blackness that I live with. It is very important to me that my husband does not feel that he is second best but I have not yet found a way of assuring this, and I fear that I never will. I want him *and* them. And I always will.

Patricia's story:

I think the empty nest syndrome is rather a pat name for a very painful feeling. However my reactions may be a little extreme as both my children went abroad to study and have not lived at home since.

My husband died in 1988 and just over a year later my eldest son went abroad to study. My second son got a place at a university in America but I was not prepared for completely falling apart when he went to the States. When my friends phoned me to see how I was I couldn't bear to speak about him. It was as if he had died, too. I looked at his bedroom, next to mine, the day he left and I knew he would never be part of my life again. It seemed to me that our little family of four had dwindled down to one.

I don't count myself as a clinging mother, but every time my children leave, I am distraught. I wander round the flat, crying and moping. Life seems empty and pointless. Perhaps if they could home for weekends or if I knew when I was going to see them next, it would be different.

The other side of this is that when they have an accident, or get into some kind of trouble abroad, it is much more difficult to help them. Even though they are 22 and 24 I still feel like this and I have friends with much older children who still feel anxious about them. You have to let them go and not make any demands on them, but you yourself do pay a price.

Nevertheless I know that my children are doing what they want, are reasonably happy and having fun. I am glad for them, but I do still miss them.

Isabel's story:

My experience of empty nest syndrome hit me when my daughters moved all their personal possessions out of their rooms and set up houses of their own. I was surprised. During the years they were at university they came and went and were away for long periods, so what was so different? I came to the conclusion that what had been removed, when they were finally adult and functioning individuals in their own right, was the underlying sense of purpose that had informed my life since their births. It was that sense of purpose that had brought them to this point.

I have a good relationship with my daughters and have just had a grandson. I am glad that they are happy and successful. That I felt so moved and terribly choked for a period by the sparseness of their rooms, denuded of the personal possessions, the owl collections, the engineering structure, one can only put down to part of life.

I lead an active life and in no way can it be described as having revolved round my daughters in their late teens and college years. I grieved when they left home for good and it was true grief, a process that had to be worked through. I came to the conclusion that this was natural and not abnormal in any way.

I loved them. True love lets them go but I mourned that loss even though I knew it was coming. I thought I had prepared for it, but you can't, not really.

These stories do not end here. The women who have felt grief, bereavement, surprise and shock when their children leave home will not stay in that place as long as they recognize that this loss, like any other major loss, requires a period of mourning and a working through of all the stages of grief. When this is accomplished they will be ready to move on.

The Devaluing of Motherhood

Motherhood is demeaned in this, the latter part of the century. We are not considered to be whole women unless we are proving ourselves in other, more recognizable ways. Motherhood is considered an incidental adjunct to the rest of a woman's life – just part of the package of career, travel, study, personal growth that has become regarded as so essential to the modern woman.

Yet consider this. Sonia, childless by choice, has worked hard on her chosen pathway and at the age of 40 she achieved her goal; she was promoted to a senior post in a well-known publishing house. The embryonic germ which eventually blossomed into this achievement, took form when she stepped on the first rung of the ladder at 25, with a job as a publicity assistant in another publishing house. During that 20 years she climbed that ladder single-mindedly, step by step. It was what she wanted to do and where she wanted to be. Sonia was happy. Her success was recognized, applauded and supported by women. She had a partner she loved, a comfortable lifestyle and plenty of friends. Sonia applied herself, heart and mind to the job she loved. Then five years later, during a reshuffle, her job ceased to exist. She was devastated.

Twenty years of work, dedication, energy and commitment, all gone. Sonia got another job, a good job, but it was not exactly what she wanted, and besides, she mourned the one she had lost. That was what she had been happy doing. Sonia's loss, though, her despair, her feeling of redundancy, was recognized – in society, in the workplace and especially among other women. This loss was seen as significant, important. And this acknowledgement by others, this affirmation that she was justified in her unhappiness helped her to pass from her depression to a more positive state of mind in which she was able to find another job and start another kind of life.

The word 'redundant' recurred time and again as women attempted to explain, or to put down on paper, their feelings about their children leaving home. One woman neatly summed it up:

| Perhaps it would be strange if we did not feel in some way

redundant once the children become independent. After all bringing them up has been a full-time job, and a very important one at that, like being a managing director carrying all the responsibility and gradually ending up as a junior, then having no job at all and no chance of finding another one like it.

Yet Sonia's experience was accorded a validity which is denied the woman grieving for the end of active mothering, though why should it be any different? Why do we recognize that no longer being needed after 20 or so years in a much loved job is somehow more important than the same feelings when our children leave home? The answer, of course, is that motherhood is considered to be of little value in our society, though whether this is as a result of patriarchy or of the rise of feminism is a contentious issue. In her classic book on motherhood, *Of Woman Born*, Adrienne Rich says:

> The woman at home with children is not believed to be doing serious work; she is just supposed to be acting out of maternal instinct, doing chores a man would never take on, largely uncritical of the meaning of what she does. So child and mother alike are depreciated, because only grown men and women in the paid labor force are supposed to be 'productive'.

It is clear from the context of Rich's book that her conviction is that the depreciation of motherhood is a direct result of patriarchal oppression. But not all feminists share her point of view. Naomi Ruth Lowinsky, a feminist psychotherapist, is deeply concerned that feminism has caused women to lose sight of the feminine principle. In her book *The Motherline: Every Woman's Journey to Find Her Female Roots*, she describes the way in which she and other newly liberated feminists distanced themselves from all aspects of their female heritage:

> I read feminist thinkers who devalued motherhood and expressed revulsion about the feminine mysteries of gestation and menstruation . . . 'Femininity', it was argued, was basically

a product of socialization and we would be better off without it. Pop psychology books scolded women for not being more like men . . . Women seemed to want to live their fathers' lives. Mother was rejected, looked down upon, left in the dark. In the headlong race to liberate those aspects of ourselves that had been so long denied, we left behind all that women had been.

This split, says Lowinsky, has created a dangerous situation for women. She describes a terrifying dream in which her three-year-old daughter's head was severed from her body and heard her mother's voice telling her that she would never get her together again. She interpreted the dream literally and lived in fear for her daughter until she attended a workshop on Jungian psychology. There she learned that the dream was symbolic; 'It was I who could not get my head and body together; I who could not integrate my intelligence and ambition with my deeper, instinctual, female life; I who felt split between the feminine and feminist aspects of my being'. Lowinsky also felt the dream represented the collective situation of women. She says:

In the generation that has passed since my son was born and *The Feminine Mystique* was published, I have come to understand that we are living out a cultural split that can be described as the feminist ambivalence about the feminine.

Gail, a close friend with whom I shared all the stages of having and bringing up children, has always been an ardent and campaigning feminist who feels that there is a war between feminism and motherhood which makes her deeply troubled. Now a successful academic writer, she feels driven to present this face of herself to the world, when really she says, she would like to give up work and be a housewife.

I can't do that, though, because I feel I would be betraying all that the women's movement has fought for on my behalf. I feel that my career is admired but my role as a mother is marginalized. I don't think women are valued by other feminists for having children. I certainly feel that no one ever

valued me for having children, yet it was the most important
thing I've ever done.

Have we really achieved liberation when women like Gail feel they
cannot give up work, should they want to? Surely true liberation is
about making choices, with the support of other women and these
choices should be unremarkable. Not so very long ago the
appointment of a woman to a highly paid executive position with
Coca Cola would have made headlines; now that same woman
makes headlines and becomes the subject of endless debate and
speculation because she chose to give up her job to stay at home
with her child. That, I think, is a poor reflection on feminism.
Women still feel they have no choice. When I was working on a
popular women's magazine I saw a great deal of conflict and
competitiveness when it came to having children. The competitive
element was who could return to work the quickest after the birth,
the conflict was that many of these women desperately missed
their children and wanted to be at home with them.

In her book about the development of feminism, *The Second
Stage*, Betty Friedan addressed the dilemmas of women such as
Gail:

> From these daughters – getting older now, working so hard,
> determined not to be trapped as their mothers were, and
> expecting so much, taking for granted the opportunities we
> had to struggle for – I've begun to hear undertones of pain and
> puzzlement, a queasiness, an uneasiness, almost a bitterness
> that they hardly dare admit. As if with all those opportunities
> that we won for them, and envy them, how can they ask out
> loud certain questions, talk about certain other needs they
> aren't supposed to worry about – those old needs which
> shaped our lives, and trapped us, and against which we
> rebelled?

In an article in *The Times* (14.1.95) journalist Ginny Dougary
gave a compelling account of the high level stress of being a career
mother. When her first child was six months old, she felt so keenly
at times that she was missing out on his childhood that it hurt.

Now, years later, Dougary works from home, with the back-up of a husband, a nanny, a mother who can be relied upon to babysit and a 'treasure' who cleans the house, tends the garden, sees to the dry cleaning and does the monthly bulk shop. Even with all this help, she finds herself questioning the quality, not to mention the sanity, of her chosen lifestyle and compares working parenthood to a flimsy 'house of cards'.

Ginny Dougary is the victim of feminist brainwashing – the notion that no woman can fulfil her true potential unless she is juggling career, partner, children and social life in a never-ending exhausting whirl. She knows this, admitting some reservations about writing the feature: 'Middle-class angst is infinitely lampoonable,' she says. What she doesn't realize is that she, and others like her, are as much the victims of oppression as were the women of their mothers' generation who were castigated if they did pursue a career when they had small children at home. The oppression has been turned on its head and the result is the same: like the generation before them, nineties career women have been made to feel they have no choice. She cannot call to mind a single woman friend who has exchanged a career for full-time motherhood, so entrenched are they in the belief 'that endless domesticity would drive them round the bend'.

I can. I offer an example: Helen, senior company executive, in line for a big promotion, dedicated career woman, single-minded, driven and rather uncertain as to whether she wanted children at all. But as the ticking of her biological clock began to impinge, she decided to have a baby, strictly on the condition that it did not interfere with her career. I went to see her when the baby was a few weeks old. She was worrying about how she would feel about leaving him when her maternity leave was over. 'Why not stay at home?' I offered. She felt that wasn't an option. Nobody stayed at home with children. What about her career? How would she survive with just a baby for company after life in a busy, stimulating environment? I said no more. I could see she was torn, but did not believe that she would seriously consider full-time motherhood – a less likely candidate I had yet to meet. I had a letter from her that Christmas, full of joy and contentment and sounding far less frenetic than the Helen I had always known.

Quite simply, she had found that she did not want to leave her son. She had stayed at home, filled her life with other things. I wondered if it would last. Then she had a second child. She is still at home, still happy, busy, fulfilled. Sometimes she misses her job, the people, the buzz, but she has never been so happy and knows that for her she has made the right decision.

Or take Marina. She worked for the BBC and their crêche provides one of the best child-care facilities. She returned to work after her maternity leave, knowing that her daughter was well cared for. But even though she could see her at lunchtime she felt torn. She didn't feel she was having it all; she felt she was having a poor half of both worlds. She talked about leaving but her women colleagues were shocked. She felt unsupported by everyone except her family, who, being Italian, did not find her desire to spend more time with her child in any way strange. She finally made the difficult decision to give up her career temporarily, and is now at home with another baby. She has investigated and found freelance opportunities and could hardly be said to be living a life of endless domesticity.

What Helen and Marina have demonstrated is that women should and do have a choice. This is what feminism has given us: the chance to have it all. Or to choose part of it. There is no longer a stigma attached to the decision to remain childless. Neither should be there be a corresponding stigma when nineties women decide on full-time motherhood. However, there is. Helen was treated by her peers with disbelief, scorn and pity. Some thought she'd lost her mind and many thought she would no longer be an interesting person to talk to and meet with. She did not receive the support of the women who juggled children and career and this speaks poorly of sisterhood where surely all lifestyles should be recognized as equally valid. This feels very male to me, as does Ginny Dougary's assumption about 'endless domesticity'.

But this surely, is where it has gone wrong? There is a conservative lobby who advocate women's return to the kitchen but on the whole there is an acceptance that society has moved on. What has happened, though, is that women have exchanged their traditional roles for *male* roles, rather than for *female* roles of power.

Women have emulated the male model and are suffering for it. As Penelope Leach observes in *Children First*:

> The women's movement has dismantled many barriers that protected men's powerful public lives, but gender equality is still defined as sameness and the model for it is still a male one.

And so women like Ginny Dougary compete for the male role and so are conditioned, like men, to repudiate the idea of 'domesticity'.

What an indictment of women's creativity, women's ability to create their own stimulating environment, which when centred round a young family does not rely exclusively on it for stimulus, variety, society. Women have an immeasurable talent for making their lives as fulfilling and as satisfying as they wish them to be. Those of us who had our children in the late sixties and early seventies left promising careers – though all my friends and colleagues from that time have resumed their careers – and we used our gifts in diverse ways during those years at home. I don't remember anyone being bored and certainly there was no sense in which we were trapped in domesticity. We learned new skills and perhaps most importantly, relied on our selves, our own sense of inner creativeness, rather than the thrust and bustle of a career out there in the world. And we returned when we and our children were ready for us to do so. I cannot help feeling that we were more fortunate than the present, middle-class generation of career women, who like Ginny Dougary are struggling to bring sanity and balance into their lives but not knowing how to do so.

Hallmark now produce greetings cards for working mothers to leave for their children when they don't see them in the morning or at bedtime. 'Have a super day at school' says one, and another 'I wish I were there to tuck you in.' Hallmark know their market; have women really achieved their goal of 'having it all' when cards like this are necessary?

It is essential at this point to be clear about what I mean by working motherhood. A huge number of women do not have the luxury of this choice; for them working when their children are small is an economic necessity – and not the necessity of maintaining an affluent, middle-class lifestyle. For these women it is the difference between feeding and clothing their children and seeing them hungry and cold. They do not have nannies, or back-up help; an article in *The Times* thoughtfully placed next to Ginny Dougary's piece highlights the tremendous stress suffered by these working women who often have to let their primary school aged children return home to an empty house while they, at work, experience anxiety about them. Gerard Sagar, of Kids' Clubs Network, one of the support groups for working parents, says: 'We also know of mothers who might have to make 15 different arrangements a year for a child: a relative one day, a friend the next, a school pal the other and so on.' And Irene Pilia, Information Officer of Parents at Work says:

> I don't think the struggle is affecting children yet. That's because parents, particularly mothers, pull out all the stops so that children don't suffer. However exhausted they feel when they get home, they put on a smile and sit on the floor to play Lego when what they really want is to sink on the sofa with a gin and tonic. But if this stress culture goes on mothers will get worn out and ill.

In a very different context, Ginny Dougary's piece echoes this. She quotes a day when the nanny had flu, the old nanny had injured her leg, her mother was too tired to help, the neighbour had just had a baby . . . and so on. They muddled through she says but:

> Will we always be able to muddle through? I have the fears, the doubts, the intermittent sense that it cannot be healthy for working parents – those of us who attach some importance to the second word – to be leading such driven, exhausted and quite often, joyless lives. Our children deserve to be more than appendages to our busy existence . . . This question of finding the right balance to our lives is fundamental and demands to be addressed. I don't have the answers. Do you?

I think the answers are beginning to emerge. Naomi Ruth

Lowinsky, in *The Motherline*, says that women are discovering
that they are paying 'a terrible price for cutting ourselves off from
our feminine roots.' She recognizes Ginny Dougary's situation:

> Women today, who have spent years working hard on their
> professional identities, are feeling empty and full of grief for the
> children they have not borne, the relationships they have not
> had. Women who 'have it all', careers and families, feel torn
> with guilt and confusion about priorities and roles.

There are signs that the climate is changing. American career
women with children are questioning the quality of their lives. In
The Feminine Mistake: Women, Work and Identity, Judith Posner
observes that women are recognizing that they have exchanged
one form of oppression for another and become caught by the
notion that achievement only exists through paid work from
which women are opting out. These women are seeking a new,
female identity and setting out to create a balance between work
and family. They are no longer defining themselves in terms of
their career. Judith Posner's contention is that women are the
primary nurturers and that the male world of work is therefore
untenable for women.

Penelope Leach looked at surveys of women's feelings about
going out to work. The results showed that women working
through economic necessity would rather stay at home if they
could afford to do so. A 1990 report by Social Community
Planning Research revealed that 64 per cent of women questioned thought that women should be at home with children
until school age. A 1992 Gallup Poll found that two-thirds of the
mothers questioned would choose to stay at home if they had
such a choice, and in American surveys spanning the years
1989–1992, nearly 80 per cent of American women said they
wished it were possible for them to stay at home and care for their
young children. This begs questions about women being unable
to face endless domesticity.

We have superb role models whose lives and achievements give
the lie to the feminist brainwash. Actress Anne Bancroft dares to
commit sacrilege and heresy when she says:

> Keeping the home is the most important work in the world,
> and if I thought of it as second fiddle, I wouldn't do it. It's not
> only first fiddle, it's the composer, conductor, the whole
> orchestra. Why? Because we got along for thousands of years
> without all these businesses made by men, without movies, but
> you can never do without the cave, the home, the fire, the
> meals. Those are the basic things that women care about and
> organize . . . Work is important for a man's identity. It's not
> that important to women. They have a choice.

Anne Bancroft talks about her various roles as mothers, from the
seductive Mrs Robinson in *The Graduate* to a middle-class British
mother in *The Pumpkin Eater* and the Jewish mother in *Torch
Song Trilogy*. She is quite happy to play mothers, observing that
there are few other roles for women her age. 'Actually', she says,
'there's very little that women do in real life except be mothers.'
(*Radio Times*, 16.11.94)

An inflammatory statement, and one that I personally do not
agree with, though I feel it was a throw-away remark rather than a
considered opinion. Anne Bancroft is a highly intelligent, strong,
powerful woman who has maintained a balance between family
and career without compromising either. Women struggling to
create some kind of balance in their lives will probably feel
immense anger, both towards me and the women I am taking as
role models. I feel strongly though that there is no place here for
censorship and if my, or their opinions seem anti-feminist, then
perhaps this is part of a swing away from the dominant male
model of work and the devaluing of traditional women's roles.

Writer Alice Thomas Ellis is no slouch when it comes to
achievement. Her novels have won major awards including the
Whitbread prize, and have been shortlisted for the Booker. She is
much sought after for her opinion on just about every aspect of
life, love and the pursuit of happiness and she has a huge crowd of
interesting, successful and close friends. For her, though, family
and friends come before work and motherhood comes before
everything. She is nobody's victim. And she is certainly not a
feminist.

The perfect couple is not, as you might suppose a man and a woman, it is a mother and child. To me, motherhood is the most complete relationship of all. I think the mother and child relationship is of infinitely more significance, infinitely more interesting than romantic love. To me, it's the whole point and purpose of life.

Feminists find this an impossible concept but only because it is currently deeply unfashionable for motherhood to be 'the whole point and purpose of life' while at the same time pursuing a career and filling one's life with interest, colour and variety. They are not mutually exclusive as Alice Thomas Ellis has so brilliantly proved.

How is it going to be for these women when their children leave home? It may be argued that they will not suffer from the empty nest because their lives have been so filled with their career. It is too soon to be definitive; the career mother as a concept only took form in the 1980s, but there are signs that some of those women who have stretched themselves beyond any reasonable capacity are paying the price. One woman wrote to me about this:

I don't know if what I have to say comes within your remit; neither of my children has yet left home. But my elder daughter is 14 now and I feel I know little about her life. She has, of course, reached that age of independence where she is striking out on her own, forging her own character, but it seems to have happened without my being aware of it beginning. They change so fast when they reach puberty and the hard fact is that I am not at home enough to witness this emerging of the butterfly from the chrysalis.

I am a senior executive in an advertising agency. It's a tough job, and particularly so for a woman. The men don't seem to mind the fact that we sometimes work until nine at night, sometimes later. They have a sense of 'If that's what the job requires, then that's what we'll give it'. And I have to work to the same principles and never show that I'm anxious because it's Friday night and I haven't been home in time to see the children before bed for days. Or weeks. Of course, now they are not in bed early but by the time I get home, they are out, or in their rooms with friends listening to music, talking, doing whatever teenagers do. They come down to make coffee, say 'Hi, Mum, you're home' and that seems to be the extent of our communication. And can I blame them? I've had to miss parents' evenings, sports days, concerts. They've got used to me not being there.

But will I get used to them not being there when they leave? When my elder daughter leaves, in about four years time, will I know her? Will I know who she is, and how we will relate when she has gone? Have I missed something important or will it not matter in the long term? I can't know the answers to any of these questions until it happens. Maybe it will be alright – perhaps what I am feeling now is guilt and some kind of nostalgia for their childhoods that I never really shared. Has it all been worth it? I don't really want to answer that question. I'm afraid of what the answer might be.

To Love, To Cherish and To Let Go

Of course the mother and child relationship continues after the child has left home, but there is a time of uncertainty and adjustment which has to take place before the relationship reshapes itself and finds a different place. And part of this change is the parting itself, and the aching knowledge that we can no longer shield our children from the world, from danger, unhappiness, rejection and losses of their own. As Alice Thomas Ellis says:

There's that awful thing of having to love them and then let them go. It's terribly hard. It's not that you want to keep them, it's that you want to know they are going to be *safe* forever.

How true. For no loving mother, however much she mourns the ending of her role, would wish her child to be stifled, kept at home through a feeling of misplaced duty, or because he or she felt it unsafe to go out into the world. No woman, seeing her sons and daughters out there, becoming themselves, forming their own lives with partners, in jobs, setting up their own homes, having children, would not wish that for them. I know 'children' in their thirties, forties and even fifties, who for various reasons have never left the parental home, and to me it seems a terrible thing, a waste of potential, of opportunity and a denial of life and growth for both parent and child. In short, a tragedy. The parting signifies a job well done, even though the price of this success may be pain. This, I thought, was poignantly expressed by Stella Clark in this poem:

Parting

I was ready for the pain of the first birth.
Almost.
I had practised, as I lay upon the floor,
Puffing, panting,
Clenching and relaxing,
Isolating parts of me
That were not needed for the birth.
Carefully preparing
For that long process
Of my baby's separation.
But when it came,
The agony astounded me
As that small being struggled free,
Until at last, with one long cry
Broken by pain past all control,
The parting was complete.
And I became alone again;
But with the birth came
Love.

And as our children
Each in turn were born,
They came into a world
That we had made for them.
Their lives were bounded by our care,
For in the safety of our arms
We sheltered them;
Trusting each other
With what we loved the most.

Each small progression,
(Source of reassurance and delight)
Was preparation for the time
We knew must come.
We watched them as they found their lives,
Saw them change and grow –
Become themselves – not ours.
Half irritated, half amused,
Stepped over leather jackets,
And great clumsy boots,
And piles of clothes,
And mugs of old cold tea,
Switched off the music playing in an empty room

The second births
Have been more terrible than the first.
For after separation comes the pain,
As I let go
What I most long to hold.
All my love and pride
Is not enough now
To protect them, as
Alone but strong,
They go into a world of others' making.

To friends who ask, we say,
'The house is rather quiet – but clean and tidy',
And we laugh.

I practise being busy, happy and content,
But in spite of all my preparation,
I cannot isolate
My heart.

(*From Women's Voices*)

In a letter to me, Stella Clark described her feelings now that her
children have been gone for some time. To me, her honesty about
her pain and her courage in letting go, sum up all that is essential
about this experience;

We have a son of 26 and a daughter of 24, both dearly loved
and I wouldn't change an inch of them. They both went to

university and this provided a graceful way for them to leave home physically and emotionally. I did become very depressed once they had both left, and it is reassuring to learn that this grieving is common among women, (and men too?)

I do have a very happy and fulfilling life, but in spite of this, I still miss our children very much. I hope to find the balance between keeping contact with visits, letters and phone calls, and maintaining a separate and strong identity. I hope my love is a positive factor in their lives, and not a negative one of feeling stifled or responsible for my emotional happiness. The greatest gifts I believe we can give our children are those of independence, emotional strength and freedom from guilt.

5 THE NATURE OF LOSS

The immediate response to loss of an important source
of positive value is likely to be a sense of hopelessness,
accompanied by a gamut of feelings, ranging from
distress, depression, and shame to anger.

Social Origins of Depression by
George W. Brown and Tirril Harris

'I know it sounds silly. But sometimes when I shut my
eyes I can almost feel their hands as they used to be in
mine, all small like children's hands are . . . Even when
they are actually with us, and grown up as they are today,
I still sometimes get these feelings of longing for them as
they were.'

'I know. Those children have gone.'

'Yes. Gone forever. It's – it's almost as if they died. Oh
dear, I shouldn't say that. I know we're lucky really.'

'Don't bother with that,' said Joe passionately. 'It is as
if they've died. I know exactly what you mean. One isn't
allowed to complain, but actually it's terrifying.' And he
thinks: Have I been so dreading that something terrible
will happen because, in the profound illogical core where
parental love has its being, I think something terrible has
already happened? The disaster of loss, unformulated
but with many possible faces, that we fugitively dreaded
all the years we were rearing the children, has, by terrible
anodyne sleight of hand come all the same. With concen-
tration and prudence and luck we avoided it . . . only to
meet it again in another guise, round the final corner.
Our children have gone. And the nice but busy and
competitive adults who have replaced them are no
substitute. It's just this: the ultimate, inevitable betrayal
of love, of care. Nothing more.'

To the City by Gillian Tindall

For me, the summer of 1993 seemed to be all about loss. My elder daughter, having spent one year in America had returned home the previous year to take up her place at university, but at the end of this, her first year, she decided that she wanted to return to the States and set about preparing to leave again. My younger daughter was getting ready to leave home for the first time, to take up her place at university. In August my best friend died of breast cancer and another close friend told me she was going to live in Spain.

So for me that summer was also about meeting that loss head on, trying not to turn away from its reality, diving into the pain and trying not to fight the changes. The ending of the summer was a drawing together of all the separate threads of that loss to make a whole: weaving a tapestry of pain and acceptance and transformation, each sensation, each emotion a different tone, mixed with the colours of summer itself, the memory of the light and sunshine forever inseparable from the love and longing and loss that accompanied it. And by the autumn they had all gone and there was a great, deep hole and I began to sink into it. I actually felt as though I were falling, I felt dull, lethargic, depressed. Eventually I realized what this loss was all about, and what loss meant, not just for me, but for everyone.

Each time we lose something, or particularly someone, it reawakens echoes of all the losses we have ever experienced and even though we may not consciously remember or associate them with what is currently happening for us, they resonate, sometimes from far back. Loss is perhaps the hardest part of the human condition and though we deal with it in our different ways, we never ever get used to it. In her book, *Healing Grief*, Barbara Ward lists the stages of grief. They are:

Shock and disbelief
Denial
Growing Awareness of feelings, including some or all of the following:

Longing	Guilt
Anger	Anxiety
Depression	Acceptance

Although this excellent book is primarily about bereavement, the author says that the above model can apply to all forms of loss. People tend to apply a qualitative criterion to loss; something like the 'There is always someone worse off than yourself' cliché. While this may well be true, it does not lessen or invalidate the powerful feelings we all experience, in whatever part of the landscape of loss we find ourselves. The hours I have spent talking with women trying to cope with their sorrow over their children leaving home and the hundreds of letters I have received full of pain, all use the language of loss and grief in exactly the same way as if there had been a bereavement, though often with the addition of another kind of guilt: that they felt they had no right to grieve because after all, nobody had died. But all these women have experienced some or all of the above emotions.

Shock and Disbelief

Two emotions very much associated with the death of someone, yet they can also be found in the woman whose role of active mother has come to an end. In some instances, it is the manner in which their children leave; many women experienced a sense of shock when their children left much earlier than anticipated, or when siblings left within a short time of each other. Sometimes the leaving is acrimonious and this brings its own kind of shockwaves and the burden of unfinished business. Disbelief, in empty nest syndrome, is a close relative to denial.

Denial

This takes many forms, some similar to those experienced when a person dies. Mary wrote:

> I keep her room just as it was when she was at home. Her posters are still on the walls and I love arranging all her stuffed toys on her bed. She's married with a home of her own now, and I know she won't need her childhood things, or sleep in her room again, but I like to keep it this way.

When I met Mary, she showed me the room. It was both pathetic and slightly eerie: suspended in time, in her daughter's childhood and adolescence, looking as though it was still occupied, or waiting for its occupant to return. But its owner was a 23-year-old woman who had 'put away childish things'. The problem for Mary was that *she* had not. It reminded me of the way that the belongings of the dead are often kept 'just so', rooms maintained as shrines, sometimes places even laid at table. I recognize this kind of denial: my father, who lived in the cottage next to us, used to visit us every evening for a chat at around eight o'clock. When he died, I remember watching the door for some time afterwards. It was as though I could bring him back by the power of thought; if I believed he was going to walk through that door, as he always had, then he would. I remember saying, unhinged with grief, to my worried husband: 'He'll be here in a minute, just you wait and see.'

Another type of denial for empty nest sufferers is the longing for the past, for their children's childhoods, for the happy times when, through rose-tinted glasses summers were always warm and sunny, family holidays were a joy and small children brought nothing but pleasure. Just as we idealize the dead, so it is easy to remember motherhood as a time when things were perfect, and to forget the reality of sleepless nights, anxieties about school, and the ceaseless demands made upon us. Browsing contentedly in a bookshop the other day, I was struck suddenly with a vivid memory of shopping with small children; not only is it virtually impossible to browse with them around, to concentrate on yourself, but I also remembered the sudden urgent demands for the loo, the frantic hurrying them out of the shop and looking desperately around because with small children, there are just never enough loos nearby! Now, my adult children browse with me in bookshops and I had not realized what a small luxury this is until I had that sudden vision.

But I understand so well how seductive this type of denial can be. If in our minds we move back in time to the days when we had our children with us, when we controlled what happened to them, and when it seemed as though they would always be with us because it is almost impossible for most people to conjure up a vision of the future – if we fix our minds upon these things, we can escape, at least in fantasy, from the reality of facing up to the fact that they are grown-up and have gone.

There is another type of denial which is related to the echoes of previous losses. It is human and understandable that when we face great pain we try to turn away from it. We put it out of our mind, we rush into displacement activity, we paper over the cracks. In short, we often do not allow ourselves to grieve. It is uncomfortable, to say the least, and some people fear that to give way to grief will somehow unhinge them; that they will fall apart, that they will start weeping and not be able to stop. We are unconsciously reminded of our helplessness as children when we had no defences against grief and when this caused us to feel naked and vulnerable, finding that not being able to control our crying led to teasing by other children, or worse. Many of us have a fear of losing control, as if by staying in charge of our emotions, by repressing them, we will be more whole, not 'cut up' or 'torn apart'. Language is very powerful in the imagery it attaches to emotions.

When I was 12, my mother had my cat put down. I went with my father to the vet and then had to return to school. In the middle of an English lesson I broke down into uncontrollable sobbing. Not only did I have the shame and embarrassment of crying so publicly, I was reprimanded for lack of self-control by the teacher and sent out of the room until I could get a grip on myself. We are all familiar with 'Pull yourself together'. I realize now that the teacher was quite incapable of dealing with a child's pain, but at the time I thought I must be weak and somehow bad. Even now, I have problems crying in front of anyone and for many years could not face dealing with any kind of pain at all. And I know this is not an uncommon experience. In this country, we are not good at dealing with grief or in supporting those who openly grieve. It's not 'nice'. It's not comfortable and most people prefer it to be swept under the carpet.

And so when children leave home, a major watershed in a woman's life, she may find other, unresolved losses coming up from the past and demanding, perhaps for the first time, to be dealt with. And the only way forward is to go with the pain.

When Julia's two children left, she found herself mourning the loss of two miscarried babies. She says:

It makes no rational sense. I never knew those babies – I lost them at a very early stage in pregnancy. They had not yet become real to me. But now I can't stop thinking of them, of who they might have been. I find myself wishing I'd known what sex they were and why I lost them. I keep reliving the miscarriages and find myself crying for them, as though I'd lost four children, when in fact it's the leaving of my two that I'm distressed about.

For Caren, it was a mastectomy five years before her last child left home that surfaced and demanded to be dealt with to her great surprise:

It's every woman's dread, isn't it, finding a lump in your breast? Well, it happened to me and I faced it well, I thought. I didn't try to deny it, I was straight down to the doctor's surgery and in hospital the next day. It was a stage two carcinoma but they assured me they could get it all out in a lumpectomy. I wasn't having any of that. I know lumpectomy is just as successful as mastectomy but I couldn't get rid of the image of stray cancer cells having broken off from the lump and running around unchecked in my breast. So I opted for a mastectomy. I was so pragmatic about it. I received counselling before and after the operation but all this stuff about being less of a woman without my breast made no sense to me. All I could see was that I had a life-threatening illness and the best thing I could do to maximize my chances of survival was to get rid of the lot. I didn't find it distasteful afterwards, I was just relieved to think they'd taken away all those rotten cells. And once the prosthesis was fitted I more or less forgot all about it. It made no difference to my sex life – I'd been married for thirty years and my husband said he would rather have me alive and minus a breast than dead with a neat little scar.

Caren put so much energy and positive thought into her rational appraisal of her situation and her conviction that mastectomy gave her a better chance of survival that it did not occur to her conscious mind that she had suffered any kind of loss.

> I had all the check-ups and my five-year clearance coincided with my third and last child leaving home to go to university. Suddenly I felt as though I'd been dive-bombed. There was this terrible, tearing grief. I wanted all the children back home again and I wanted not to have had cancer. It was the first time I'd tried to deny what had happened to me. I thought it was something to do with the combination of children growing up and intimations of mortality which were heightened by the fact that even though I was in the clear, I was well aware that the breast cancer survival rate is not great. And I think those factors did come into it. What was so peculiar though, was that what seemed to be at the heart of my grieving for the children was that I would never breast feed again. I knew this made no sense; after all I had never intended to have more children. I went to see a counsellor who specialized in helping breast cancer patients and she helped me see how much buried grief I had for my lost breast. It was terribly painful to deal with because I'd done such a good job of convincing myself that losing the breast was the best – no, the only option. I'd never had any patience with those women who talked about feeling incomplete after a mastectomy. I thought they should be grateful to be alive, as I was – and I thought that was all that mattered. Now I see that losing my children and losing my breast were bound up together and facing the loss of all of them started the healing process.

Longing

This is a powerful component of the grieving process in empty nest syndrome as much as in bereavement and this, too contains elements of denial. The longing is usually focused in some sort of wish to turn the clock back; for it, whatever it is, not to have happened. It is a gut-deep pain without words to express itself easily. It is what women feel when they speak of looking at their children's old toys, or when they find the silence unbearable, when they wander into empty bedrooms that no longer have that almost tangible presence, or when they cannot bear to see the school bus. It can be quite shockingly raw. In relation to empty nest syndrome, we have to be watchful that it does not turn into a selfish longing because to want our children back is to deny them their own lives, the culmination of that part of our role as mothers.

Longing can also take the form of wanting that time over again so that we can do it better, get it right with the benefit of hindsight but this, too is a treacherous feeling. Mothers are suffused with guilt but the fact is that we have done our best and that is all our children want from us. This feeling of not having 'got it right' is very close to regret; it is important that we do not get stuck in a place where we cannot let go of the past because of our convictions that we could have done it better.

Anger

I had often read about people feeling angry with a dead person and could never understand it; after all, I reasoned, they could not help dying. When several close members of my family died, I was encouraged to express my anger towards them for leaving me. I simply did not understand nor feel such a thing. But when my closest friend died, the anger hit me. She was so strong, so invincible, so capable. How dare she let death get the better of her and leave me without a best friend? And I know now that this strange reaction is extremely common.

Anger is part of grief and in any loss it is a natural and understandable part of the process. The woman who feels adrift when her children leave may find apparently inexplicable feelings of anger welling up; anger at the children for leaving her, anger at fate, anger towards herself for not being able to deal with the situation. Often this anger is taken out on a husband or partner; they are there in the firing line and therefore an easy target. The man may feel assaulted by an anger for which he can see no cause, and unless both partners are aware that this anger is a necessary part of the grieving process, there may be difficulties in the relationship.

The important thing here is to acknowledge and accept that however bewildering it feels, anger is normal and to experience it is not wrong. What matters is what we do with the anger.

However, anger in empty nest syndrome can be complicated and unpredictable. I was concerned for some women who talked to me about their angry reactions to their children leaving home. They felt their children should not have done something which precipitated them into such unhappiness and they found it hard not to express this towards their children. This tended to lead either to feelings of guilt on the part of the children, or more commonly, to a distancing, amounting to alienation which caused great sadness and in some cases, bitterness.

My friend, Ruth, who is a wise and experienced psychotherapist, explained how anger can be cloaked by blame and hidden by depression:

Often people blame the source of their unhappiness, but until one can give up blaming what has happened, or who has apparently made it happen, one can never become reconciled to what it is that has happened. One can never forgive the person for dying, or yourself for letting them die, or the hospital – and as long as there is blame around, and as long as women are blaming themselves, even unconsciously, there is no resolution. They have got to be able to feel angry – whether it is with circumstances beyond their control, with others, and with themselves. That's the most difficult, being able to be angry with oneself because it means you've got to take responsibility and if you can't do that, you can't express anger and you will be depressed. When I see depression I always ask 'Where's the anger?'

There are ways of dealing with anger. Some people find it helps to let rip, to scream and shout in an empty house or car; maybe to a sympathetic partner or friend. Counsellors often recommend some form of activity, such as painting out the anger, or kneading bread dough, punching and pummelling it – this can be extremely satisfying and takes the edge off the power and rawness. It doesn't matter, as long as it is directed somewhere harmless and as long as it is not suppressed. And however hard it is, we should not direct our anger at our children who are doing what is right and normal for them, however painful it may be for their mothers. It is perfectly possible to feel anger without blame.

Depression

Depression is about emptiness, bleakness, despair. It can take the form of copious weeping or of not being able to find the release of tears. Some people find they want to sleep all the time, some cannot get to sleep; some cannot eat, some turn to comfort eating. There is sadness, loneliness, loss of confidence and self-esteem, feelings of hopelessness and pointlessness. Often the sufferer finds it difficult to believe anything will ever be normal again.

Many of the women who suffer empty nest syndrome express some or all of these feelings. Some of them are aware of their depression, many are frightened and bewildered by it. It is important that people know that feelings of depression are another natural part of loss and the grieving process and that it is not necessarily an illness.

The following poem was given to me by a woman who sank into a deep depression when her last child left home:

> ### Hell and High Water
> I didn't know it had been raining.
> Shut off from the world
> In a cold shell of isolation,
> But the water rose around me
> As the ground could not absorb it.
> Cut off from the world,
> Huddled, hidden,
> Curled up like an embryo,
> Not hearing or seeing,
> But still. Still, lest a movement
> Should send pain rushing through me
> With its armoury of knives,
> Jagged blades, numbing blows,
> Pushing me down into the blackness,
> Into the dark depths,

Like drowning
At the bottom of a cold grey sea,
Sinking, reaching out for a hand,
But no loving touch meets mine.
Then surfacing
And returning my body to the everyday.
Uncurling, unfolding.
No pain now.
Heart death.

Going out, the moors are flooded.
Too deep to turn back,
Something else that had to be got through.

I didn't know it had been raining.
Today I have been through hell and high water.

For me this poem provides a vivid illustration of the power of depression, though that could be said to be a purely subjective response. And so because I am not an expert on depression, I turned to one. Tirril Harris is a Research Fellow at London University and her specialist area of study is women and depression. Her book, *Social Origins of Depression*, co-authored with Professor George W. Brown, is an illuminating and analytical study of women's depression, its causes, its nature and its treatment. What I learned was that there are 'vulnerability factors' which predispose to depression – and the principal one of these is loss. The authors describe events surrounding loss as 'the deprivation of sources of value or reward' and suggest that 'what is important about such loss for the genesis of depression is that it leads to an inability to hold good thoughts about ourselves, our lives and those close to us'. In other words, self-esteem is lowered and often barely perceptible. It is clear from Brown and Harris' work that low self-esteem is a primary factor in depression and my own research shows that many women suffer low self-esteem when their children leave home because of the feelings of redundancy they so often express. These emotions are often accompanied by a sense of something that is almost paralysis; certainly at this stage these women find it difficult to feel positive about anything. As Brown and Harris put it:

> Feelings of hopelessness will not always be restricted to the
> provoking incident . . . It may lead to thoughts about the
> hopelessness of one's life in general. It is such *generalization* of
> hopelessness that we believe forms the central core of a
> depressive disorder.

These feelings of hopelessness, say Brown and Harris, usually
occur in response to some external change. For many people,
change, and fear of change is psychologically synonymous with
loss, even though change may present opportunities for growth
and redevelopment. Brown and Harris recognize this:

> With change we risk, at least temporarily, losing the sense of
> life's reality . . . crises may raise fundamental questions about
> our lives. They focus our attention on the present and since
> this is the visible outcome of our past – our choices,
> commitments and mistakes – we may come to question what
> our life might have been, what it is about and what it will
> become. A son leaving home may produce for his mother
> alarming thoughts about the hollowness of her marriage and
> how she is to cope with it without him. Indeed, anticipation of
> change may be enough – simply news that her son is proposing
> to emigrate.

One woman in Brown and Harris' study felt that the onset of her
awareness of the loneliness and pointlessness of her life dated
from the time her 16-year-old daughter returned from a summer
holiday. 'I missed her', the mother said. 'When she came back she
was much more grown-up and I felt that I had lost her and I
could realize then for the first time that one of these days I would
lose both of them. It made me realize just how lonely I was and
how I depended on their ways'. Brown and Harris record that
this woman's assessment was 'not unrealistic. A major depressive
disorder followed soon afterwards'.

The following account illustrates well how losses can build
upon themselves to create a state of hopelessness and despair that
is in fact depression:

I wonder how often it happens that you end up with a kind of 'multiple empty nest syndrome'. For me it started 12 years ago. First my elder and much loved son married and left home to live abroad. A month later, completely out of the blue, my husband left with just a few weeks to go before our silver wedding anniversary. He returned home and left again twice, within short periods of time. Each time he left my pain was unbearable. After he finally moved out – into the arms of a younger woman, of course – my home was burgled and I lost so very much – all the gifts of love over the years from my husband, my sons, my departed mother and grandmother.

This was a tremendous added loss to bear. My younger son was still at school and on completion of his college course he returned to live with me. At this point, I had to move to a smaller house and sell a lifetime's possessions. After several jobs, my son was sent to Brussels but returned every few months for weekends. Each time his going was very hard for me, but I coped fairly well. The first time he left was very traumatic although most of his things remained in his room and I did not feel so alone. Last year his work in the Brussels office was finished and he returned home. However, he had met a Belgian girl there and she was preparing to join him so they could live together in London. A few days ago, he finally left home. His room is stripped and empty but I have not yet had the courage to look inside. The pain is too great and there is a constant dull ache in the region of my heart. The past years of what appear to be never-ending losses have certainly taken their toll and although I pick myself up, dust myself down and carry on, I have been told – and I know it's true – that I no longer smile very much and my eyes look so sad. In a way I am lucky as I have an excellent job; I visit my elder son and two adorable little grandchildren in California once a year which is a compensation but also a difficulty when I have to face the farewells again. I am due there for my annual visit now, but once again I am dreading the return to an empty house. I can only say now that I have nothing left that could possibly affect me any more.

Betty, the writer of the above letter, makes an important point
when she talks about 'multiple empty nest syndrome'. The stage
at which our children leave home tends to coincide with other,
difficult life events; financial problems, redundancy, support of or
death of elderly parents, menopause, hysterectomy. A number of
women raised this and spoke of how these extra pressures or
losses compounded their feelings of sadness and grief:

> Coinciding with my children leaving for college, I underwent a
> hysterectomy. Although I was 45 years old, I grieved
> unreasonably for the fact I could never bear another child (I
> hadn't planned on having a third.) At this time my husband
> retired early. My life changed totally in the span of only two
> years and I was finding it difficult to cope. Compounded by all
> this we began to lose people close to us – my husband's
> parents, a dear friend, our neighbour (in an accident), two
> cousins (in an accident). I thought I was heading for a
> breakdown. When I finally, in desperation, consulted my
> doctor she was adamant I needed HRT. I am now on it and
> feel considerably better, but I feel I would not have plunged so
> deeply into despair if it were not for the hysterectomy. I
> personally don't think my despair was specifically on account of
> the children leaving home, but a combination of circumstances
> at that time, ageing parents, bereavement, retirement,
> menopause.

> As soon as our children left home and the immediacy of
> parenting was gone, we thought that our time would be our
> own, but we discovered that as soon as we stopped worrying as
> parents, we started worrying for parents.

> I was pleased when both my children went to university and
> decided I would do something for myself, so I started on a
> part-time degree. Then a series of bereavements occurred for
> which I was not prepared. I am sure this frequently happens to
> people in their fifties just as they are making a series of
> adjustments to their lives. First my father, then my mother,
> then my father-in-law all died within the space of six months. I

had very good relationships with all of them without being dependent on them and I thought I had managed to cope with their deaths.

However five months later I started visiting my GP. I was obviously a familiar case to her – I had experienced a series of life events and reactive depression was the result. Because I was determined not to take the prescribed Prozac I then embarked on a series of alternative/complementary medicine treatments, including reflexology, homoeopathy and hypnotherapy. Very expensive.

Nearly a year since I started visiting my GP I feel that I am recovering, though with hindsight I wish I had recognized that self-help is not enough. I also needed good, supportive and constructive advice, and above all, someone constant to listen to my worries and fears – not to be found at my doctor's practice. I found that my husband was eventually bored with my problems and said he could not help. I felt that I couldn't continue to burden friends, who would look at me and say that I looked and sounded quite normal.

Although anxiety and stress are very common and not something you die of, they can also have a devastating effect on one's life at a time when one is most vulnerable. Trying to cope on one's own is both frightening and exhausting – one needs all the help one can get.

In *Social Origins of Depression*, Brown and Harris observe that:

Recognition that loss plays an important role in depression, has of course, been widespread. While a good deal of the extensive research literature has dealt with death, Freud made the point in *Mourning and Melancholia* that the object need not necessarily have died but simply have been lost as an object of love.

Furthermore:

For a woman who has earlier lost an important person by death, the emigration of her child may be seen to have death-like qualities.

This was borne out by a series of letters I received from a woman deeply afflicted by just such an event. Dorothy, whose first letter to me conveyed great distress, felt she had coped well when her first child, a son, left home to get married at the age of 22:

> I felt sadness, yes, it was the end of an era, and the beginning of a new time in all of our lives. I was also a little anxious as I thought he was rather young to be getting married – and I have to admit to a little jealousy of his future wife, though I understand that this is not uncommon amongst mothers of sons. He settled down and we saw him and his wife fairly frequently. I welcomed her as a daughter-in-law and worked at establishing a good relationship with her. I do think we are close now.

Three years later, Dorothy's remaining child, her daughter, left home for university. Dorothy found that she experienced feelings of sorrow and loss, but came to terms with this and adjusted to life as a couple again. Her husband was considerably older than she was and towards the end of her daughter's first university year, he suffered a stroke and died.

> I was completely devastated. Even though he was older, he wasn't old and I had imagined we had many years ahead of us. We had begun to settle into a comfortable way of life, not demanding anything of each other, enjoying being together, both learning to get used to the quiet house – and I must say, at times finding the peace rather nice. But when he died – oh, I wanted it all back. I wanted my family around me. I longed to ask my daughter to come home again but of course I didn't. I didn't tell either of the children how desperately lonely I felt. It was not my place to burden them. And they were missing their father desperately too – I had to support them in their grieving. Very slowly I began to come to terms with being alone, with the help of Cruse (bereavement counselling) and some very good friends. I think I was dealing with the stages of grieving and it helped to know what they all were and that they were normal.
> When Kate graduated she had a New Zealand boyfriend

whom I had met and liked very much. They were in the same year at university, though not reading the same subject. I had no idea the relationship was that serious – maybe I just didn't want to see the signs, I don't know. Two weeks after their graduation Kate broke it to me that they wanted to get married and that Jake, her boyfriend, wanted to return to New Zealand. I couldn't take it in. I simply could not face it. I went through the next six months completely numb as they made their preparations to leave. I know Kate felt dreadful but it is her life and I kept reassuring her about that. When I saw them off at the airport I was almost out of it – a friend had given me some Valium and I'd had an awful lot to drink.

I didn't come to terms with her leaving. It was completely irrational but I kept feeling as though she were dead. I felt I'd been bereaved again but it didn't make sense. I couldn't talk to anyone about it. My life changed completely – I stopped wanting to go out, I couldn't eat – there seemed to be no point. I couldn't sleep properly and I felt all the time as though I was wrapped in a stifling grey blanket through which I could neither see nor feel. There really seemed to be no point in anything and I wondered how many more days, weeks, months I would wake up every morning and find the same bleakness, that awful feeling that here was another day that I had somehow had to get through.

After several months of feeling like this, Dorothy went to her doctor. He recognized that she was quite severely depressed and prescribed a course of anti-depressants. She was lucky in having a wise and compassionate doctor who not only recognized that her depression was caused by undealt – with grief but who was prepared to give her the time to talk about it. She discovered that the normal process of grieving for her husband had been aborted and suppressed when her daughter went abroad and that in fact, her daughter's leaving was like a second death for her. Now that she has begun to mourn both these major losses, she is beginning, slowly, to come through. She says:

I know now that I will get better. Ken has gone and Kate will

probably not return but I can go and visit her; in fact I've got a
trip planned for this summer. The most important thing for me
is that now I can feel hope for the future. When I was very
depressed and didn't realize it, the really frightening thing was
the feeling – more than a feeling, a conviction – that there was
nothing left for me. Now I realize I have many fulfilling years
ahead, probably grandchildren to look forward to, and my son
and daughter are happy and healthy and we are all close. It's
terrifying to think I came so near to wishing my life was over.

There is constant debate as to what constitutes clinical depression
as opposed to 'depressed mood'. George Brown and Tirril Harris
agree with Aaron Beck, psychologist, the founder of cognitive
therapy, who 'has described its (depression's) central core in
terms of the self seeming worthless, the outer world meaningless,
and the future hopeless. From a medical perspective there are
internationally recognized guidelines for the diagnosis of depression as a clinical condition; the following are the main symptoms:

1 Depressed mood which occurs nearly every day and lasts for
most of the day; feeling sad, empty or tearful.

2 Loss of interest or pleasure in almost all activities, nearly
every day and for most of the day.

3 Change in weight; either loss or gain.

4 Sleep difficulties; insomnia, waking in the night or very early
in the morning, or sleeping or wanting to sleep for much
longer than is usual.

5 Feelings of physical or mental agitation and/or feelings of
being slowed down, sluggish.

6 Fatigue or loss of energy nearly every day.

7 Feelings of worthlessness and/or guilt; loss of confidence
and/or self-esteem.

8 Diminished ability to think or concentrate, indecisiveness.

9 Recurrent thoughts of death or suicide.

*(Sources: International Classification of Diseases, WHO,
and The American Psychiatric Association)*

The consensus among clinicians is that if five or more of the above symptoms have been consistently present for more than two weeks, a diagnosis of depression may be made. Treatment is likely to be with medication – there is now a wide variety of different types of anti-depressant; with counselling or with a combination of both. If you feel you may be suffering from depressive illness, don't be alarmed. There is no stigma attached to depression, though there is still a regrettable tendency among some less sensitive individuals to think that depressed people should pull themselves together, or be 'jollied out' of their depressed mood. Depression is no more a person's 'fault' than is a broken leg (in many cases, less so!) and taking medication for it is no different from the diabetic who injects herself with insulin.

During the course of their thorough and extensive research, George Brown and Tirril Harris found that one of the principal vulnerability factors predisposing to depression was the absence in a woman's life of a confidant. This can be a husband or partner, a mother, other relative or a close friend, but the hallmark of the confiding relationship is that a woman feels she has someone with whom she can share all her problems, feelings, worries, doubts and joys with complete trust and with no fear that she will be judged. Many of the women who shared their stories with me reported that they had not been able to talk about their feelings to anyone. Many of them said their husbands could not understand their sadness, and that friends whose children had also left home seemed to be coping well, or not feeling the same sense of loss, redundancy and bereavement.

It is clear from many of the accounts I received from women who are suffering empty nest syndrome that their sadness and feelings of loss have been compounded by a very real depression. It is academic at this point to speculate whether their feelings constitute clinical depression or depressive illness. While the symptoms I have listed above provide a useful guide to the diagnosis of depression that might otherwise have gone unrecognized, any woman who *feels* depressed can ask her GP for help, whatever her symptoms. The problem is that many do not feel that they have the right to do so. Women who suffer when their children leave home often get into a downward spiral. Society tells us loud and clear that we must let our children go; if we do not do so, we are bad mothers. If we mourn, if we feel depressed, we may believe we are not doing a good job, we feel guilt and shame and often keep silent about it. If we are sad, lonely and weeping we feel we have failed as good mothers and therefore do not see the validity of our feelings; consequently we do not consider ourselves worthy of help from any source.

This was made apparent to me by so many of the women who spoke or wrote to me. 'This is the first time I have been able to express this', was a statement common to many. Remembering the importance of Brown and Harris' 'confiding relationship', it is worth considering whether there is a relative or friend who would meet the criteria for this; it may prove well worth the risk of breaking silence. But whether or not the confiding relationship is present, any woman feeling depressed can take the first step towards healing by reassuring herself that she is not alone, or abnormal, or a bad mother; that she needs support and help and that she deserves to ask for it from her doctor or from a coun-sellor. It is perhaps relevant here to remember that what we are talking about are the features of grief and that grief which is not 'worked through' can turn into depression. The grief which over-whelms some women when their children grow up and leave is likely to be an accumulation of previous losses and sources of grief which have not been dealt with; the whole being triggered by this 'last straw' event which constitutes such a major life change. Addressing this in a therapeutic context may be painful but it will ultimately heal more than one kind of wound. It is the only way to move on: as Brown and Harris put it:

The concept of 'working through' grief is central; it is the process by which alternative sources of value can be found and accepted, and by which hope can be revived.

The loss of hope, which is such a major feature of depression is destructive to the soul. No one has to live with it; the help is there.

Guilt

'Guilt thy name is woman' and if women in our society are the bearers of guilt, how much more so are mothers. Expectations of good mothering are imposed upon us from all sides and yet motherhood itself is denigrated, given no status in our culture. No wonder it is suffused with guilt. And when our children leave home we may feel guilt that we are not celebrating their coming of age with unrestrained joy; guilt that we feel sorrow and sadness and perhaps a lot more; guilt that we are not raring to go into the next phase of our lives and guilt that everybody else appears to be achieving, and coping – without guilt! These feelings come from our ambivalence about our children leaving home. Barbara Ward explains this extremely clearly in her book *Healing Grief*. She says:

> Often guilt comes from the mistaken idea that it's wrong to let go of old relationships. I think each relationship we have is a learning experience. Once we've got the lesson we either need to deepen the relationship – explore new aspects – or move on. This doesn't mean the relationship wasn't important at the time, but like an old garment, you have outgrown it. You no longer have the same things in common: your lives have gone in different directions.

And with our children we have to learn to move on from our relationship with the child to a new relationship with the emerging adult. The previous dependent relationship is over, and it is more helpful to reflect on what we have learned from that part of our mothering than to feel guilty for our shortcomings.

And because we are expected to be good mothers, we lay this burden upon ourselves too. At the time our children leave, all the things we have done wrong, real or imagined may come back to haunt us and the most trivial incidents can fill us with guilt. We feel it is our responsibility to send them out into the world equipped with values, skills and coping strategies and we are inclined to berate ourselves for not getting it right.

At a dinner party recently, we were all asked which decade of our life we would choose to relive; one woman said it would be her thirties because she felt so guilty about her mothering that she would like to have the chance to start again and do a better job. In the perception of everyone there, including me (and I had known her since her children were babies,) she was a wonderful mother, but the incident captured the ingrained feelings of guilt that so often is the lot of mothers. In the process of looking back down the years, as our children move on into adult lives, we remember things that we want to wipe out. When my first daughter left, I looked back through her 18 years and came upon a tape I had made in which she, aged five was practising her newly acquired reading skills. At the same time her three-year-old sister, not to be outdone, was loudly 'pretend' reading from one of her story books. My elder daughter was quiet and introverted, the younger one an extrovert performer!

To my horror, I realized all those years later that my attention was mainly focused on my three-year-old's demands that I listen to her 'reading' while the elder one read quietly to herself with just the occasional query. Now I can see that it was in fact extremely funny, but when I played the tape after so many years I felt guilt, and wondered if I had damaged my elder daughter by my lack of attention to her need. She is the first to laugh at such an idea but it is an example of the way guilt can get us by the throat over the most unlikely and – let's face it – irrelevant matters.

Working mother's guilt is another familiar intruder at this time. When my son was six I went to work for the BBC and cannot quite rid myself of feelings of guilt and regret that I did so, even though my mother lived with us and I was often at home with the children on account of my odd working hours, many of which seemed to be in the middle of the night. At the time I remember carefully considering the decision to work and I believe it was the right one, but the trap is so easy to fall into. Many women have spoken to me about this; this is one example:

My son, who is my only child, has just left home for university and I feel immense sadness and emptiness at his going. What seems even worse though is the massive amount of guilt I am suffering because I worked from the time he was a small baby. I didn't do so through financial necessity; I had a job I loved on the local newspaper and he had excellent childcare. I did feel twinges of guilt at the time; it wasn't as commonplace for mothers to work then as it is now, but it didn't seriously affect me. I felt that I gave him all the love and attention he needed and he certainly seems to have grown into a well-adjusted young adult. But now he's gone, I keep thinking of all those years as wasted – I'll never have that time with him again and I didn't realize how precious it was. I feel I deprived him of his birthright – his mother's care and attention, at least for the first five years of his life – and I have this unshakeable feeling that I'll be punished for it, that he'll go away completely or something.

I'm not usually an irrational kind of person, but this guilt has really got to me and if only I could have my time again, I would not work.

The point about guilt is that it is made up of 'if only' and 'it's too late'. This woman did what was right for her at the time and from her account, it was right for her son as well. Child psychologist Donald Winnicott, recognizing the impossible burden of trying to be a good mother, developed the concept of the 'good enough mother'. And this is what we are. We carry out our mothering to the best of our ability. Thinking of motherhood in this way gives it a sense of perspective and can free us from those feelings of inadequacy and guilt. A friend says she wants inscribed on her tombstone 'She did her best' – she has the right idea!' Most thinking, reasonable and caring mothers flinch from the pushy parent whose goal in motherhood is to urge her children to excel in order, though she would not admit this, to shower her with reflected glory. Just as the pushy parent is destructive to a child's wellbeing and balance, so perhaps are the impossibly high standards we try to impose upon ourselves as mothers. In *Healing Grief*, Barbara Ward sums up guilt succinctly:

Guilt is generally about events that are perceived to have happened in the past, or that sometimes could happen in the future . . . The 'if only' of guilt is usually about us not being prepared to accept the loss.

I believe this ties in very accurately with the guilt that accompanies empty nest syndrome. In our inability to accept loss, we reach back and try to retrieve and remake the past, to try and comfort ourselves in a perverse way by thinking how much better we could do things if we had the chance. In reality, though, we are just beating ourselves with an extremely big stick.

Anxiety

The landscape is suddenly unfamiliar; the routines, the patterns of the last 20 or so years have disappeared. We have to map out a new territory for ourselves and it is not surprising that anxiety is a part of this. While some face the prospect of change with anticipation and excitement, many more feel apprehension and uncertainty. In some ways, there are similarities to the beginning of it all, the time when we embarked upon parenthood and our lives were changed, the territory was unknown, our previous roles altered. We did not know what to expect or what we would become or whether we would be able to cope. If we assume that parenthood was planned or at least accepted, it suggests an element of choice. But after the 20 or more years of parenting growing children, the outcome is out of our hands.

For the purposes of this book, I would add Confusion to that list. Bereavement is a recognized part of our culture and there are clearly defined reactions and milestones in the process. For the woman feeling grief when her children leave, there is no model in society for her to relate to. How much harder it is to grieve for something that everyone says is natural, especially as part of the confusion lies in the fact that not every woman does experience empty nest syndrome. Many pass effortlessly from this to the next stage in their lives, leaving those who do mourn in a state of even greater confusion, laced with guilt.

What is it That We Have Lost?

It is relatively easy to identify the more tangible aspects of our children's absence; the silence, the unfamiliar tidiness, the lack of young people's company; their vitality, their need to argue and discuss, their lively presence. Grown children are exhausting, often demanding, high-handed, rebellious and headstrong but many mothers find the teenage years stimulating and rewarding, even if often frustrating. Time and again women echoed each other as they spoke of missing the thunder of heavy feet on the stairs, the sound of loud music, even the traces of cigarette smoke or the sweet smell of a joint. In our house it's known as the 'Doc Marten syndrome'. Alice Thomas Ellis says:

> I've always kept open house for the children's friends. When they got to about 14 and started behaving badly, their parents would sling them out and I would have them here. People still come and go. The fashion now is that once the kids have left home, you and your husband are left together alone. Dreadful. I believe in the extended family.

And when they have gone, when the silence and the finality have to be faced, the echoes of the past haunt us, play tricks and we lose sight of where we are. Our role, once so clearly defined, becomes blurred, unfamiliar – we still have children but the nature of motherhood has changed and the parenting of an adult child is so very different from that of young children. And as the landmarks disappear, many women look back and cling to the memory of the familiar and desperately want to return to it:

> Usually at this time the house is bustling and noisy, the 'phone is going, music playing – and the house feels alive. I can't get used to how quiet and empty it is. I have got my own interests but all I really want to be is a Mum and do all the mothering things I used to – picking them up from school, taking them to Cubs and Scouts and music lessons, their birthday parties, chatting with their friends. Now I feel aimless.

Women feeling like this are expressing a sense of dislocation, a sense that the landscape is alien, that the familiar markers that give their lives shape and form have gone. They do not know where they are and most important, they do not know *who* they are.

Role Identities

I miss our grown-up children so much. When I visited my younger daughter in her new home in London, I broke down in floods of tears. The sudden closeness of her had triggered a waterfall of emotions which I could not stop. My husband and my daughter were puzzled and didn't understand what was going on – I just wanted to hold my daughter and tell her how much I missed her. She asked me what the matter was but I couldn't find words – I didn't know what it was myself. Later I realized that it had been her new flat. She was so self-contained, so at home there. She'd found it by herself, she'd decorated it, her things were all new, none of her old stuff from home; it was all so unfamiliar to me and that is when I realized that I no longer knew what my role as a mother was any more.

The last few words of Teresa's letter, above, to me encapsulate at least part of the nature of the loss experienced in empty nest syndrome. We are a society in which roles are an extremely important part of the structure of our lives; they are how we define ourselves and how we mould ourselves into each different facet of our particular lifestyle. Here I propose that motherhood is more intrinsic to us than any other female role because it is biologically determined. Whatever cultural and personal factors influence whether and when we have children we cannot deny the driving force of our own biology. Metaphorically I have my head well below the parapet when writing this for I can hear the enraged outcry of feminists. But a large proportion of the stories entrusted to me are from *feminists* who thought it would never happen to them, because motherhood was a chosen role in a whole chain of chosen roles.

What these women lose, as well as the company and presence of their children is their sense of who they are; their role and iden-

tity. This is a complex matter, perhaps least of all understood by
the sufferers themselves who are well aware that they have other
roles. As one woman said:

> I am a mother, yes. But I am also a partner, friend, career
> woman, daughter, sister. I'm the feminist voice in our rather
> reactionary local women's group. I'm the oboe player in an
> orchestra and one of the few altos in the church choir. I am
> conscious of my various roles – I feel I take on a different one
> with the change of clothes that goes with each of these very
> different identities. How, then, can I feel such a sense of
> displacement? Mothering my children is the only one of these
> identities that seems real, as though the others are just things
> to fill in, to mark time. Yet my life is so full – why am I so
> empty? Why does the void left by the cessation of one of these
> roles seem so big that the other things I do cannot seem to
> close over it and fill it?

I think that what this woman is saying is of vital importance. It
indicates the key to the nature of role identity, which is more
about who we are than what we do. If a woman is unsure of the
essence of who she is, as opposed to what she *does*, no amount of
activity or number of roles will fill the gap in her psyche where her
only certainty is her identity as a mother. 'What I do', said one
woman, 'is working as a vet, cooking and entertaining for my
husband who is a businessman, playing squash on Thursday
nights, seeing friends, going to the theatre. But who I *am* is Jamie
and Hannah's mother.' It is a strange sort of split, the conflict
between *being* and *doing* and it is one that needs reconciling in
order for healing and progress to take place. We need to look at
both how we define ourselves, in our own eyes and in the eyes of
society, for an essential part of wholeness is that our definition of
ourselves, in identities other than as mothers, should have a real
and tangible validity. Only then will we be able to incorporate the
role of mother into the many parts that make us the women we
are. As Adrienne Rich puts it so well in *Of Woman Born*:

> Motherhood, in the sense of an intense, reciprocal relationship

with a particular child, or children, is *one part* of female process; it is not an identity for all time. The housewife in her mid-forties may jokingly say, 'I feel like someone out of a job'. But in the eyes of society, once having been mothers, what are we, if not always mothers? The process of 'letting go' – though we are charged with blame if we do not – is an act of revolt against the grain of patriarchal culture. But it is not enough to let our children go; we need selves of our own to return to.

Tirril Harris, co-author of the book *Social Origins of Depression*, with whom I spent many productive hours discussing the meaning of empty nest syndrome, succinctly encapsulated the heart of the matter. 'If you have an empty self,' she said, 'you will have an empty nest.'

This set me thinking about the concept of self in relation to motherhood and I realized that the word so often used in the context of good mothering is 'selfless'. Much praise is heaped on those who are selfless; certainly mothers are expected to be so, but analyse the word and what does it mean? Surely it means without a self; here is the clue to the complete loss of identity that some women experience when their children leave home. Their selves are not bound up in the other roles; their selves have been fully invested in their children.

In her excellent book *The Motherline*, Naomi Ruth Lowinsky considers the trap of selflessness. Referring to the liberating influence of Betty Friedan's *The Feminine Mystique*, which, says Lowinsky, 'empowered women to see the cruelty of the projection that women should be selfless' she goes on to remark that:

We began to understand that lives lived only to meet the expectations of others were hollow and meaningless; such lives robbed us of identity and direction. Like a woman whose breath and life energy are constructed by tight corseting, our true selves were constructed by the psychological girdle Virginia Woolf had named the 'Angel In the House'. Trapped in the cultural expectation that, to paraphrase Woolf, we become intensely sympathetic, intensely charming, that we sacrifice ourselves daily, that we never have a mind or wish of our own, all that was original, creative, and full of spirit in our natures was crushed.

I want to make it very clear here that this is not true of all empty nest sufferers, for there are always degrees of sadness and pain when children leave home and I maintain that much of this is a natural, predictable reaction to loss. It is when women feel that there is no future for them, when they no longer have children to mother actively, that the concept of the empty self needs to be considered. Valerie, a sad, depressed woman of 60 told me:

> I've definitely lived for my children. My whole life has been centred round them. I always saw them as the number one thing in my life and me as coming second. I miss them so much. I feel as though my life is over – the best part of my life has definitely gone.

For women this is a time of transition and these tend to be vulnerable times. Women at this life stage may need their confidence boosting, as they pass from their most familiar role to what can appear a frightening and empty landscape. The following account illustrates well the aridity of this transition combined with the dawning of understanding that the safe and familiar role must give way to a new and different identity:

> It's hard to explain, it's as if you've for the past umpteen years subjugated your whole life for the sake of others, and on receiving it back, don't know what to do with it. Unsure of what role you are now supposed to play, you are left with an awful lot of this person that you don't really know. I used to work evenings, so all day long I became this stranger who didn't know what to do with the hours till tea-time when, once again the familiar woman would take over and do what she had to do. Safe back in the niche she was used to.
> 　　I took to catching a bus into town and wandering aimlessly around the big stores. They're impersonal, you see, nobody is going to look twice at a middle-aged woman looking at bathroom suites, or carpets, and there are so few staff that you

can wander for hours without attracting any attention. I got into the habit of sitting in the cafeteria after my wanderings, drinking their insipid coffee and smoking cigarette after cigarette, my brain in overdrive, while I desperately tried to figure out what on earth I could do with myself.

A man used to come and sit at the next table, and after seeing me there a few times, started talking to me. The usual sort of things, the weather, the coffee, just small talk. He was a lot older than me, an ordinary sort of man to look at. He was working on the new superstore being built nearby, tiling the bathrooms on show there. He was a nice ordinary person, easy to talk to – I felt none of the pressure with him that you sometimes feel with men you don't know. It turned out that his wife had died when she was young, leaving him three children to bring up on his own. They had left home now, so he was able to work away, which gave him more money. He had such a positive attitude that he made me feel silly to take the girls leaving so badly.

I eventually told him why I was always sitting there. He passed no comment except to say 'Time for you to be your own person now'.

My own person. God knows what a frightening thing that was, a mother since the age of 17 and now at 38 no longer 'Mum' all day, but Dorinda.

In her novel *Lost Children* Maggie Gee focuses on the role identity of the mother and how drastically that can change when something unforeseen happens to a child. Alma, the central character of the book, appears to fall apart when her teenage daughter Zoe disappears. Suddenly Alma is no longer sure of who she is at all and she leaves her husband and has little time or patience for her son. The novel follows Alma's obsessive search for her daughter, which leads her to look back down the years for meaning in her own life. It is an uncomfortable, sometimes painful story, as she discovers a buried memory of childhood abuse by her father whose blond looks her son has inherited. In the course of her discoveries, she loses sight of who she is – she would rather forget that she is a daughter to her parents, she cannot relate to her son or husband and she feels she has lost her role as Zoe's mother, the one role she desperately wants to rediscover, but she does not know if she will ever see Zoe again. I liked Angela Neustatter's perceptive review of this novel (*The Independent*, 5.4.94) which addresses the question of the role identity of middle-aged mothers. She describes Alma as 'cracking apart like a ripe oyster' when Zoe leaves home – an apt metaphor for the loss of purpose felt by many empty nest women in less dramatic situations:

> This abrupt ending of her role as mother, as the person with an immutable sense of purpose and worth sends Alma spiralling into a crisis. Her dilemma is typical of that suffered by many middle-aged women. What is it, after years of secure routine, that makes a woman crack? The triggers can be many and varied: children leaving home, or suddenly finding herself peering at a partner who has come to represent utter tedium and wondering 'Is this it?'

Judy expressed this same loss of role and purpose, despite knowing she was still needed and still active:

> When my son left home suddenly, five years ago, I wandered into his room, missed him, missed having someone to mother, to wash, cook and clean for. Yet I still had a husband, a dog and a mother-in-law living at home. I was still needed so why did I feel so bereft? Then this year my dog and my mother-in-law both died and the empty nest syndrome has got me with a vengeance. I'm trying to be positive and I've filled my time with training to work for the Disabled Information Advice Line (Dial). I'm also doing a writer's course and I work part-time, but if I sit alone the pain comes back to haunt me. I wake in the night thinking doom-laden thoughts and I feel as if a stranger is in my body.
>
>   I have a theory that for a while, sadness affects the body's defences, creating some sort of mental reaction which affects our physical well-being. Is it all downhill from here, for women? We've had our children, we're losing our looks (well, I am) and anything I do to alleviate my distress is really only superficial.

Is facing it the answer? Should we stop the cover-ups and the fill-ins and accept our situation. Not as easy as that, is it?

No, it's not easy. But the first steps in moving through loss are the words in Judy's last paragraph: 'facing it' and 'accept'.

There is a time to grieve and a time to move through grief, to leave it behind. The following words, written by a woman who had previously said she could not articulate her feelings about her children leaving home, poignantly capture the essence of this major change in a woman's life:

That autumn. The garden covered in leaves, the bare trees and the rooks' nests. The two of them, a struggle, internal, visceral. Let go. Leave the past. The house, full of light and warmth and noise. Music. The moon shining through my window. People coming and going, then going, only going. Panic. Absence. Tension. Merciless. Resolution. Standing at a threshold, move, cross over. The light and the darkness which was never dark but blue, midnight blue. Time, fear, change, loss. Transition then peace. A completion. The ending and the beginning of love.

6 LETTING GO: RELATIONSHIPS WITH ADULT CHILDREN

The mother-child relationship is paradoxical and in a sense, tragic. It requires the most intense love on the mother's side, yet this very love must help the child grow away from the mother and become fully independent.

Erich Fromm

That dear octopus from whose tentacles we never quite escape, nor in our innermost hearts ever quite wish to.

Dear Octopus by Dodie Smith

The empty nest is about more than one kind of change, one type of loss: it also represents the inevitable shift in relationships between parents and their adolescent and adult children. Our children need to separate themselves from us in order to become who they are meant to be and this process starts in the teens, often in the form of defiance, rebellion and apparent rejection of the values and standards we have given them. For many parents this is a difficult and bewildering time as teenagers appear to turn into monsters, unrecognizable as the children we thought we knew. Most of us have known the slammed doors, the hours spent in their rooms rather than with the family, the arguments, the sullen silences and the breakdown in communication when language seems an entirely inadequate medium for making contact with these strangers. Parents know they are regarded as dinosaurs with no valid opinions and many feel quite battered by the experience. The young person's struggle for the assertion of self can take many forms, largely dependent on their upbringing and their parents' views and feelings. For instance, a very conventional friend of mine was distressed almost to the point of mortification when her daughter dyed her hair purple and dressed as a Goth. Not being very conventional myself, I rather liked the idea of this break from orthodoxy; consequently none of my children ever attempted any kind of unusual appearance. But this is the whole point; for them to have done so would not have constituted any kind of rebellion. They found other ways!

This is an important stage, a foreshadowing of the search for autonomy and individuation which will eventually help them to shape their adult selves, and the parents' role is both crucial and difficult. We have to find the balance between allowing them to develop and find their own ways of being, and guiding them, for they are in need of guidance still, however much they may scorn and refute such an idea.But that rejection is in the nature of the separation from us. At this stage our influence and that of teachers and other adults is a vital factor in determining which values they will accept and integrate for the future and which they will scorn and deny. Most parents have clearly defined ideas of right and wrong and often these conflict with those of our teenage children. Arenas of antagonism may include sex, drugs, going out (where, with whom, how late?), personal appearance, manners, schoolwork and friends.

What has this to do with the empty nest? Simply that the quality of the relationship between parents and children at this stage can lay the foundation for the time when they do leave; to try to get in touch with teenagers at this point can create bonds which will survive physical and geographical separation.

I talked with Hugh Jenkins, who is Director of the Institute of Family Therapy and a wise man indeed. He made the following suggestions for successful parent/teenage relationships:

> Make sure you are not involved with your children's lives to the exclusion of your own; you are a person in your own right as well as a mother. This is important for the children as well as for you. They need to see that you have a life of your own, whether this involves work or hobbies.

Take an interest in the things your children are involved with, even though they may not be your personal taste. Listen to their music (not all the time!) and watch some of their television programmes – Hugh Jenkins says he got quite hooked on *Eastenders* this way. It gives you points of contact and paves the way for common interests in the developing adult relationship.

Listen to your children. Communication is of the utmost importance. Be aware that the experiences they may tell you about will probably be radically different from yours at the same age. Each generation of parents deals with offspring born into a different world – Hugh Jenkins says he has it on good authority that the generation gap is at least seven and a half thousand years old! But we can try to close it by being open-minded and not showing disapproval of their chosen lifestyle.

As children grow up, the nature of the responsibility for what parents can or cannot do changes. There is a point where you cannot and should not strive to influence your children, even if you have to watch them making mistakes.

Talking to people who are going through, or have experienced this phase, it became clear that the main difficulties parents had concerned the last two points – remaining open-minded about their children's lifestyle and standing back. The first is, as Hugh Jenkins points out, the result of our children inhabiting a different world with different values and unfamiliar mores. What if they smoke? Do we let them smoke in the house? What about cannabis? And alcohol? And sex? Here is a random sample of experiences:

I know I was wrong, but when my 17-year-old daughter asked if she could have her boyfriend to stay, I went wild. I could not bear the thought of her having sex under my roof even though I knew she'd be doing it in the back of the car. She's 21 now and never talks to me about sex and I can't help thinking that if only I'd been able to bring myself to accept what she was doing, it would have built a bridge between us. But at the time I couldn't do otherwise. It's easy to be wise after the event.

My two teenagers, 15 and 17, asked me quite openly what I thought about them smoking dope. They said it was non-addictive, not half as bad as cigarettes or alcohol, which plenty of adults indulged in, and that it was a myth that it led to the use of hard drugs. I didn't know what to say but in the end I turned a blind eye. I knew they would do it anyway. I just begged them to make sure they were getting it from a reliable source and that it wasn't 'doctored' in any way. Now they are both at university and it appears that smoking dope is as commonplace as drinking tea. As far as I know, neither of them has progressed to other drugs – I can only hope and pray.

You may think this is trivial, but my son, who is in his first year at university, has joined the Young Conservatives. We are lifelong Socialists and I cannot believe this has happened. To my astonishment, he says that quite a number of the young people there are Tories – I blame Thatcherism. I don't know how to communicate with him on this. How can I show an interest in something I believe to be inherently evil, and I do, even though I know that's a strong word to us? He knows how much we disapprove and I'm afraid it's driving a wedge between us.

I had a very conventional and conservative upbringing where appearances were everything and a lot of this rubbed off on me. My daughters were always dressed neatly and tidily when they were children and their hair was kept well cut and brushed. When my elder daughter was 15 she became a punk. She dyed her hair green and had a Mohican and rings through her nose, the lot. I wouldn't go out with her, I was ashamed when people came to the house. Then a friend said to me 'If you're not careful, you'll lose her. She's only trying to establish some sort of identity and they're so insecure at that age.' I realized she was right – after all, what was the point of these constant rows over something as relatively unimportant as appearance? She was a lovely, sweet-natured girl and doing well at school. So I tried, really hard, to accept this as a phase. It wasn't easy, it really went against the grain, but it worked. I even found I could joke about it, say things like 'What colour is it going to be this week – purple or pink?' Now she's 25 and as conventionally dressed as I ever was!

Hugh Jenkins' point about standing back and not assuming too much responsibility for our children's actions and decisions was the other factor most parents found difficult. Dilemmas involved letting them borrow the car (can they be trusted to drive carefully? Not to drink? Not to show off?); being concerned about the friends they made (she's in with a bad crowd, I'm afraid they'll get her hooked on drugs); making A-Level and career choices (He'll never get physics, he should have done chemistry); she's applied to read psychology and she's not in the least bit interested in human nature; he's decided not to go to university but to get a job and he's making the most terrible mistake; and relationships (she's marrying a paraplegic – I know it will end in tears but you can't tell them, can you, they won't listen); he's going out with a girl who's as hard as nails (I know she'll break his heart).

Some parents are fortunate in their ability to let their young offspring develop as they will. These are the parents who have few, if any expectations, though there can be another side to too much liberalism. Teenagers need boundaries – they need us to stand back, but they also need us to help them develop limits, without which their world can become out of control, chaotic and frighteningly insecure.

And so we pick our way through the minefield of these years, wondering if we will ever again have an encounter with our children which isn't confrontational – and then, magically, usually somewhere between 17 and 19, they change. They enter a different, more secure phase, not adult, but with definite signs that adulthood is burgeoning. They become reasonable. They appear to have some concern for us and their families, they notice that there is a world around them that doesn't focus entirely on themselves and their peers. They become our friends and just as we are enjoying the fruits of our efforts, it is time for them to leave. Our job is done, the last and the most difficult part of it behind us and we can be forgiven for having regrets that it is at this point that we must lose the daily contact with our newly adult children. As Virginia Ironside put it:

> Every year, from the moment they are born, children seem to get more and more lovable, more entertaining, cleverer, and kinder. Then when they reach their peak of charm, they scamper off. (*The Times.* 6.4.93)

Children who leave around the age of 18 to 20 are usually going to university, or some other kind of training course. However it has become increasingly common for them to have a 'gap year' before they go, a year in which they prepare themselves for life on their own, and set about the process of gaining some maturity. Most seem to use this time for travel; there is a wide variety of projects which will take students abroad to work and to earn their keep. Those that do not follow a specific programme of this kind have usually saved, from doing weekend and holiday jobs, and make their way to India or Australia – somewhere that has caught their imagination, where they have dreamed of going.

This last year at home can be a fraught one for parents and children. The pressure of A-Levels looms, university interviews are taking place, conditional offers made and arrangements for the travelling year are under way. It is impossible not to look ahead, to realize that the months and weeks are passing quickly. And there is anxiety, understandable anxiety – on the part of the parents because their child, who may only have travelled to Europe on an exchange trip and maybe not even that, will soon be wandering somewhere thousands of miles away, out of reach for months. Underneath, children, too, may be feeling anxious about such a great leap and mixed with anticipation and excitement, this can create a stormy few months. It is at this time too, that they may further try to loosen the ties with their parents, and can seem dismayingly distant at a time when we want to enjoy the last few months of the closeness of their childhood.

And then they have gone. There is a feeling of 'never again' about it, a knowledge that this is a farewell to the child we welcomed at birth, the completing of a cycle. It is painful because we do not yet know what the next cycle will be like, what shape and character it will have and what it will mean to us and to them. I saw my elder daughter off to America, waiting with her at the airport, the five of us making desultory conversation as we waited for her to be called. What do you talk about when you are saying goodbye? Then she had to go. She walked down a passageway, waved, and in the split second just before she was out of sight, I felt the cutting of the cord. I felt it again when I left my younger daughter in her room at university. There is only so much time you can take to help them unpack and settle in. There is a very definite moment when it is time to go, you sense it and so do they. You have to leave them and in doing so, you leave part of your self and your life with them. That parting – the ritual letting go of the child, knowing that never again will that child return – has been described to me by so very many women; women of different age, class, temperament and background, all sharing one common experience:

We left her sitting on her bed in the hall of residence – she seemed paralysed. There was noise all around, people in the kitchen. 'Go and make a cup of tea, you'll meet people,' I suggested, but she felt too overwhelmed, too shy. My husband said 'Come on, we've got to leave her to make her own life now' and inside I cried out. She looked so young and vulnerable and suddenly she seemed like a little girl again and it seemed all wrong to be leaving her like that. I cried all the way home. Now, a year later, the students who live in that corridor with her are the closest friends she has ever had. She has loved her first year and is much less shy. I think you either sink or swim at university.

My son wanted to work in computers but did not get into university. When he was 19, he went down to London, sure that he would get a job (we live in Derbyshire). He did, on the very lowest rung of the ladder in a computer firm. I suddenly realized that he would have to live there. I couldn't take it in – he'd only ever known the countryside round here. We found him a bedsit, a grotty one as he wasn't earning much, and tried to make it homely for him. I can't describe how I felt leaving him there – it was the Wicked City as far as I was concerned and he didn't know a soul. He saw us off back home on the train and as I waved I had this dreadful fear that I would never see him again. And in a way, I never did. That was the last day of his childhood.

My daughter got married when she was 21. I liked her fiancé a great deal and was happy about it. We grew very close over the months we were planning the wedding. We'd never really shared anything before in the way we shared that. I suppose our relationship hadn't been that close. I was silly really – I never stopped to think that the wedding meant that I would be losing her, I was so caught up in all the excitement. It went really well and I felt so proud. Then she changed into her going away outfit and it began to sink in. I can still see her, laughing, trying to get into their old car while being showered with confetti, and then they drove off. She waved and waved until they were out of sight and I was sobbing into her bouquet (I can't remember why I was holding it). I realized then that she was his wife first and my daughter second. She was grown up and somehow I hadn't seen it coming.

My son had always wanted to join the army. I had difficulty coming to terms with this because I am a pacifist and hated the idea of him being taught to fight and to kill. I supported him, though, because it was what he had always wanted. He joined up at 18 and suddenly there was this man in front of me. I kept thinking of all the Army slogans about making a man out of you and felt it was too soon. When he left, he didn't want me to take him. He wanted to start out fully independent, so I saw him off on the train, in his uniform. It was a terrible wrenching feeling. I felt 'they've got you now' and all I could hope was that the values I had tried to instill into him would still count for something. But that moment, the train pulling away, took my child from me.

I work in a university admissions office and I had always felt very impatient with parents who seemed so upset when they brought their sons and daughters on their first day. I thought how ridiculous it was that they were so often in tears, and how that wouldn't help their children at all. Then my daughter went to university and it was my turn to be a parent taking her there, leaving her in her hall. And I was devastated. It seemed such a huge parting, even though I knew she would be home in the holidays. And I must admit, I wept. I am much more sympathetic to parents now!

I will never forget that final moment of separation at Heathrow Airport and then watching the Air-India Boeing 747 speed down the runway and lift off into the heavens beyond. It was, without doubt, quite the worst moment in my entire life. My youngest son was quite inconsolable and even my normally stoic husband was quite overcome with emotion. Only my eldest son could see calmly and objectively that this was the beginning of a most wonderful adventure for Ian and that we should let go gently and be truly happy for him.

The following poem, by Dot Stokes, speaks to me of the poignancy of that moment when a parent has to let go:

How Often Should I Do My Washing Mum?

'How often should I do my washing Mum?'
The car sped on
Like a thousand others containing students, hurtling towards
The tower block in the sky.
Silence for a moment
As years of upbringing
Culminate in an answer
For which there is no answer,
It's for you to decide now son,
Test the water,
You're on your own.
'Well, feel it, smell it, see what it looks like'.
YOU make the judgement now.
Too late to say more

As we join the trail of ants,
Waving their bits of sustenance
Above their laden backs,
Bringing remnants of home life
Interspersed with stereos and washing racks,
Jostling and jangling to their new homes,
In the sky.
'Oh, it's much nicer than we thought'.
Surrounded by greenery,
A tall tower
Of window squares, stands
Outlined with concrete,
Like a noughts and crosses game,
Waiting to be filled,
Diagonally or otherwise,
Connecting new friends
Across the divides.
Teddies wave from the windows
As faces stare out,
Mesmerized.

'Well, kiss your Mum and have a good life son'.
It's up to you now,
We brought the extension lead,
And the duvet,
And the kettle,
And the washing rack,
Some stamps and a phone card (I wonder why)
And leave without an outward tear.
What more can we do?

'How often should I do my washing Mum?'
It's up to you now son,
You'll have to decide.

And so we return to a childless house, or one in which family posi-
tions will have shifted so that other children move up a place, and
we begin the important, complex and sometimes painful business
of parenting an adult child. That child, is, at this stage, a mixture
of uncertainty and confidence in his/her newly acquired independence and adulthood. They may not admit to the uncertainty,

so it is easy for parents to receive mixed messages. On one hand, these young adults are telling us that they are now in charge of their lives; on the other, they still need the benefit of our acquired wisdom and experience. The relationship at this point is a delicate balancing act and it is so easy to get it wrong. They are likely to resent anything they interpret as interference and misunderstandings can arise over the most well-meant parental suggestions or advice. The nature of the relationship at this point is that it is undergoing change, often fairly rapidly, and this makes it unpredictable.

One cause of dissent and misunderstanding can be parents' expectations. It is relatively easy to identify the more obvious ones – that they will work hard, if at university, or do well, if in a job. But there is a subtler kind of expectation that we are usually not aware of and it concerns the process of separation. We may make assumptions – that they will phone regularly, that they will visit when they can, that they will want to stay in touch with us as much as we do with them. But it does not always work out like that. Very often they do keep in touch frequently at first. They have not yet become fully integrated into their new lives and links with home are comforting and necessary. Then just as we are enjoying the fact that, though they have gone, we still get frequent letters, phone calls and visits, the pattern may change. They are too busy to write letters. They don't need frequent phone calls. They may decide to stay in their university town during the vacations. All the things we thought of as certainties – the contact, having them home in the holidays – may disappear. It is easy to feel rejected, especially as they may also appear to lose interest in things going on at home.

Rosemary was one of many women who wrote to me expressing the hurt and bewilderment many parents feel at the apparently uncharacteristic behaviour of their children:

When my daughter left home I found her 'flight' very traumatic. She went to university two years ago and the only word I can find to describe my feelings is 'bereavement'.

We have always enjoyed being together as a family and we have happy memories of holidays and outings, when the four of us were united in a loving, caring relationship. Rachel and I also enjoyed shopping trips together – days by train to London being the most memorable.

Rachel is very independent and I am relieved that she is able to cope with life in a large city after being brought up in our tiny village which is a very close-knit community. We provided her with a car to encourage her independence, and to make travelling with her belongings easier to cope with. I missed her dreadfully at first, but I kept my tears to myself and time is a great healer.

However, there has been a sad change in our relationship. She no longer wants to do things together as a family and refused to come with the three of us on holiday this year. I worry about her travelling alone on motorways, but only once in two years has she phoned to announce her safe arrival at the end of a 3½ hour journey. I have had to console myself with the saying 'No news is good news'.

On the credit side she and her brother enjoy going out together and she talks openly to him about her life in college. My husband and I do not enjoy this privilege. As we both work, she is not eligible for a grant and she is completely dependent on us financially. I wonder whether, inwardly, she resents this, and if her off-handedness is an effort to try and prove her independence to herself.

A year ago my mother died. She had been ill for some time so my sense of loss was spread over many years. In the weeks and months after her passing I did not know whether I was grieving for her or my daughter.

I hope that when Rachel's student days are over, and she is really independent, our relationship will return to what it was a few years ago. I love her dearly and I am cautiously optimistic that there will be a reconciliation.

This letter demonstrates what so many women find, especially with daughters – that the old mother-child relationship has to break down, sometimes quite brutally, in order for the newly forming adult one to take its place. It is usually our children who instigate this process, and their apparent lack of need for us or interest in what we are doing with our lives can add quite painfully to the feelings of loss of role that some women experience at this time. How do we relate to these aloof young people and what *is* our role at this point?

This is a hard lesson, for often it seems as though they are continually moving the goalposts. You may get used to their phoning sporadically but you console yourself with the thought that the holidays will soon be here. Then they ring and say they won't be home, they are going away with friends, or staying to work in their university town, or travelling abroad. And while all this is going on, you may have friends whose children appear to phone every other day, or come home several weekends in a term or always appear in the holidays.

It is worth getting a perspective on this, because here, comparisons truly mean nothing. There are several reasons for this variation in our grown children's behaviour. For example, if you live in London you are more likely to see your children at this stage than if you live in the country. London is likely to remain the home base because everything is there. Several of my London-dwelling friends still have their grown-up children living with them for economic reasons. If their children have their lives, friends and jobs there, it makes no sense for them to go and find accommodation at great expense if their parents' home is large enough. For children brought up in the country, though, their first experience of a large town can be a heady one. My younger daughter leads an exciting life in Brighton; she loves its energy and vibrancy. When she comes home to the Somerset countryside, she relaxes in its peace for a couple of days, but this is what she has known all her life, and for an energetic fast-living young woman it holds few attractions for any long period of time. She knows she will return to it and live in it when she is older but for now, Brighton is the centre of her universe.

It is important, too, to take into account the personality of the child. One friend's daughter, also brought up here, is a homebody. She didn't want to go away to college but she did so, and has done extremely well. She comes home at every opportunity because fast living is exactly what she *doesn't* want. She loves the peace and quiet of the countryside and she is the first to admit that she is a stay-at-home. Her brother, on the other hand, disappeared up to London and has hardly been seen or heard of since!

What we should be aware of is that if our children leave home and are happy and well integrated into their new lives, it is to our credit. Only secure children can leave home in this way, because only secure children know that however long they stay away, or forget to write or phone, home and parents will be still there, unchanging. It is the best gift we could give them, the security to go off and immerse themselves thoroughly in an exciting new life. However much we miss them, how could we not be glad if they are enjoying life so much?

The secret, it seems to me, is not to have *any* expectations at all. Parenting at this stage has to be a hands-off process but it is not easy to get it right all at once and it is made even more difficult by the fact that young people of this age are largely unforgiving of their parents' mistakes. They do expect us to get it right and can be quite harshly critical when we fail to do so. This can set up feelings of guilt and 'bad mothering' in the woman who does care greatly about 'getting it right'. I think we need to heed the words of Naomi Ruth Lowinsky in *The Motherline*:

> The truth is that we are bound to fail our children by our own human limitations. We need to be people as well as mothers; we will always be balancing our own needs against those of others. We are certain to err on the side of too much or too little control, discipline, love, support, attention, money. We are doomed to fail the ones we love the most.

This is a universal concept of failure and should therefore not be used by an individual with which to beat herself. Once we accept that we will make mistakes and can learn from them, we can get on with the business of being what the psychologist, Donald Winnicott called a 'good enough mother'.

Failure is important for another reason. As Dorothy Rowe observes in her book *Breaking the Bonds*, we have to fail our children, even to the extent that they feel rejected and betrayed when they are still small babies. If we do not fail them, if we were to meet their every need, they would not grow and develop or explore themselves or the world, and they would not learn the skills necessary to deal with the world. And conflict is necessary:

> What we need are not Perfect Parents, but parents we can outgrow so that we can return to our parents as friends, adults and equals. To achieve this we need to go through a period of rebelling against our parents, not just in the teenager way of doing things our parents disapprove of, but in looking very closely and clearly at our childhood and from two perspectives, that of the child we were and that of the adult we are now . . . Out of such a review we can see our parents as the ordinary people that they were and the kind of people they have become, for as adult children we often persist in seeing and reacting to our parents in the way that we did as a child. In such discovery we might also find forgiveness.

We also need to be able to free ourselves from the huge burden of guilt laid upon us by a society which *demands* that we let our children go without clinging, without weeping, without actually *feeling* anything at all. In a powerful chapter in *The Motherline* called *Wrestling with the Mother*, Lowinsky writes tellingly about the conflict that is part of the separation or 'individuation' process, observing that this wrestling doesn't fit with the 'official version' of how we should be as mothers.

> We shouldn't 'need' our children; we shouldn't 'merge' with our children except when they are infants; we shouldn't let our messy feelings leak all over our children's development. We should raise them to become separate individuals. We should have firm boundaries, always know what is them and what is us, and never intrude our personal desires into their lives. The fierceness of maternal feeling is taboo in our culture because it threatens our cultural sacred cow: individuality.

And yet we need to let go, because we live in a culture where our children *do* leave home and we have a responsibility to make it safe for them to do so. The secret, it seems, of passing smoothly into this new phase, is being open to change in whatever form it presents – and the most crucial part of change in this context is our ability to let go. This is an act of faith and of trust; it means accepting that our grown-up children may do things that concern or worry us, but if we let them find their own way they do respect us.

Perhaps it may help if we understand the meaning of the 'letting go' process for both mother and child. Our adult children are crying out to be recognized as such and we have to learn to redefine the meaning of mothering. 'What parents should aim for', says Hugh Jenkins, Director of the Institute of Family Therapy:

> Is the negotiation of an equal relationship in which parents leave children to make their own mistakes. The process of leaving home should be a reciprocal one. Children need to know that their parents have lives and activities of their own – that they are not necessary to their parents' survival. If the message coming from the parents is that it is somehow not safe to leave, there is obviously a problem about letting go. Children can be burdened by this and be unable to feel free to live their own lives.

The child who leaves home and starts a new life without this kind of burden is demonstrating that we have done our job well, though sometimes the price of that success may be pain. Is it burdening them to tell them how we feel? I believe that it is natural and understandable for us to be able to say 'I miss you' as long as there is no subtext, no hidden agenda. Children are very quick to spot 'guilt tripping' by parents. The nature of the communication in which we engage with our children is all-important. We cannot dissemble – they will know. This calls for a kind of honesty which is not always easy to achieve because it means acknowledging our failings, yet that is an essential part of the new, adult relationship.

It means recognizing that our children have opinions that are worth listening to; that in some areas they may show greater wisdom and knowledge than we possess, for their experience of the world is different from ours. Perhaps the most important aspects of this new, equal relationship are respect and trust on both sides. We have to avoid making assumptions that we will always know the answers because of our greater experience, and respect that our children's answers may be different from ours and yet equally valid. Taking the stance of 'I know best because I'm adult and you still have a lot to learn' inevitably alienates young people at this stage.

But equally, they themselves have to learn to respect us too; part of becoming adult involves joining the adult world whose ideas, values and opinions they may previously have scorned. This building of a relationship is a two-way process. Both parent and child have to learn to trust, to recognize that failings do not mean failure but are an integral, natural part of any vital relationship. And both need the capacity to say 'I was wrong – I'm sorry' – and to forgive, without feelings of smugness or triumph, when the other person gets it wrong. Love does mean having to say you're sorry.

The Importance of Peer Groups

There is another and very important development phase around this time. As each young person starts his or her independent life they will meet new people, make new friends, at university, at work, in social contexts. These are the first friends that are not connected with home and they become a powerfully strong group. They are all out there making it on their own, and they need each other at this time more than they need us. These peer group bonds can for a while seem stronger than family bonds and it is essential that we know that this is a normal process and not a rejection of us. Their group has more relevance to their lives but in no way do they replace us. As one woman, who had learned hard lessons about the letting go process said:

> Finding it hard when our children leave home may indicate that we have been short-sighted about our children and their future, that we have not prepared them for independence, that we do not acknowledge the gulf of years and experience that separate us, nor recognize the importance of them finding their own way, particularly through peer support.

There is another side to the gaining of independence and the development of their own individual way of living – and that is that it can be difficult if they need to come and live at home again. A friend whose son and daughter are both about to graduate at the same time has heard from her children that they would like to return home to live while they try and get jobs and get some savings behind them. 'I have to admit' she says, 'that I am not at all happy about this. Much as I love seeing them, they have their own lifestyle now and we have ours and I foresee fireworks.'

Magazine editor Janice Bhend has experienced this and admits it is not the easiest thing for all concerned:

Just like boomerangs, they keep on coming back, though I have experienced the empty nest briefly and intermittently. Losing your children to the adult world is painful anyway, and maybe it's made worse when they keep coming and going. You just get used to them not being there when bang, the bathroom's awash with discarded towels and talcum powder and the fridge is full of tofu and fresh chillies again.

My sons are now 24 and 22. The elder went to university, went abroad, came home for a few months and went away again to work as a Community Service Volunteer for six months. Then he got a job in London and came home, defensive about his independence and fairly broke, but intending to find a house share with a friend. Eight months on he was made redundant and he spent a miserable four months job hunting, and alternating between excitement at being shortlisted down to the last two, and despair at being rejected once again. It was not an easy time for any of us. Once you've lived away from home, it is very hard to come back and fit comfortably into other people's lifestyles again, even if the other people are your loving and giving parents. A casual enquiry, 'How did you get on today?' is interpreted as interference, a thoughtful 'Have you eaten?' seen as a gross infringement of space. And to be fair it is difficult if not impossible for parents to bite back those unwanted words of advice against mistakes being made which we see as bestowing the benefit of experience!

This is part of the reality of our children leaving home. My own daughters say they cannot cope with our unheated house in winter, even though they happily grew up in it. You have to remember that it is your house, your lifestyle and bite back the apology for any shortcomings! I just tell them to stop dressing as if for midsummer and give them hot water bottles. These conflicts are healthy, though. They are further evidence that the right kind of separation has occurred, and in time, when they are fully established, home becomes a desirable place to spend some time.

Mothers and Daughters

There are whole books written about the endlessly complex mother/daughter relationship and I cannot do it justice here. I feel it is important to touch on it at least, for the individuation and separation process is so much more intense than with mothers and sons. Women tend to see their daughters in their own image, however unconsciously, while daughters struggle to assert their own womanhood as being as different as possible from their mothers. In Naomi Ruth Lowinsky's superb book *The Motherline*, she observes this process with great insight in the chapter called *Wrestling with the Mother*:

> Many mothers identify with their daughters so profoundly that any difference is extremely difficult to navigate, while their daughters insist ferociously that they are absolutely different from their mothers.

And Adrienne Rich, in *Of Woman Born*, perfectly captures the struggle against symbiosis in which mothers and daughters engage:

> There is nothing in human nature more resonant with charges than the flow of energy between two biologically alike bodies, one of which has lain in amniotic bliss inside the other, one of which has laboured to give birth to the other. The materials are here for the deepest mutuality and the most painful estrangement.

Janet talked to me about her relationship with her daughter. Melanie is a musician, a cellist and when she was about 14, Janet was determined that Melanie would make it to the top. She herself had always wanted to be a musician and had nurtured any signs of talent in her children:

Melanie started to do really well, playing in the county youth orchestra as well as the school orchestra. I really pushed her, I was aware of it but I felt almost demented. It was so important to me that she should succeed. She was very compliant and didn't seem to mind how many hours I made her practise. I was glowing. Then she did her GCSEs. She did pretty well, but she only got a Grade B for Music. I was absolutely furious. I screamed at her and made her take the exam again the next year. She got an A. They said at her school that she was reasonably talented and might get into university to read music but that wasn't good enough for me. I wanted her to go to the Royal College, nothing less. During her last two years at school, she worked like mad and improved so much that her teachers thought she had a chance of getting in. She was changing, getting sullen and silent but I thought it was the pressure of A-Levels and music practice and would be the same for everyone. I didn't realize that she and I were getting very distant, I was so caught up with her achievement. She did get into the Royal College. And she left after a week. She wrote me a letter telling me that I had ruined music for her, that she had never wanted it as a career but I had pushed her. 'Ever since I can remember' she wrote, 'you have been there, running my life for me. I was too weak to stand up to you and besides, I didn't know then that it wasn't what I wanted. Now I see that you were just trying to make me all the things you failed to be. I'm not like you. I'm now learning to be me and I think whatever that is, it's likely to be very different from what you wanted.' She's now living in a squat and I haven't even got her address. I worry about her constantly, night and day and I don't know what to do.

Janet's story is at the extremes of the mother/daughter struggle

and has clearly defined reasons why the relationship has, for the
moment, gone wrong. Yet Janet still cannot understand why she
and her daughter have become estranged. 'I only wanted the best
for her' she says, a cliché that will resonate with many parents and
one meant in all, conscious, sincerity. But part of letting our children grow to be who they really are is accepting that our ideals are
not necessarily theirs and their values and standards may appear to
differ vastly from ours. Hannah encountered such a struggle with
her elder daughter who, while still living at home, developed a
relationship with a boy whom Hannah felt at deep gut level was
'wrong' for Mary. He was a New Age traveller, unkempt, unem-
ployed and apparently unprepossessing. She could not help make
her feelings known to Mary; apart from anything else, Hannah
had received a strict, upper-middle class upbringing and hoped
Mary would find a boy who would fit in with the family. So the
two women circled round each other, with tension mounting.
Then Hannah and her husband went on holiday on their own:

> We'd had a lovely restful week fishing in Wales and arrived
> home to find everything much as usual. Then I noticed an
> envelope propped on the dresser in our elder daughter's
> unmistakeable neat handwriting – I think I knew what it
> contained before I opened it. She told us briefly that she had
> given up her job, cleared her belongings out of her room and
> had moved in with her boyfriend. She knew we would feel
> upset but hoped we would meet them both when we felt able.
> Looking back now it seems quite ridiculous that I felt as
> absolutely devastated as I did about such a very commonplace
> occurrence. Obviously the manner of her leaving was hurtful
> to say the least but, in the light of past discussions on the
> subject, not too surprising.
>   It felt almost like a bereavement. I could not get over it. I
> would lie in bed writing letters to her in my mind – fortunately
> never sent. I would have no one but our immediate family and
> one or two very close friends told about it in the hope that it
> would only be a short time before she came home to us again.
> We made no contact with her. My husband knew that the hurt
> was still too fresh for me to behave very rationally with her.

Eventually it was she who made contact with us, on her father's birthday. The meeting was strained but it did open the door a little way . . . We had further meetings but I could never even mention the boyfriend's name so our conversations were always limited. I did ask her to come home on one occasion – make a fresh start, her teenage years had been fairly stormy ones – but to no avail. I bitterly blamed myself for what had happened. I had been too strict, expected too much, particularly morally. I myself had been fairly strictly brought up and convent educated. A friend and I had discussed how, when we married, we would be wearing white for the right reasons. How unrealistic 20 years later to expect the same of youngsters growing up in the 80s.

We settled into a better relationship and gradually people asking after our daughter were told the truth, though I can remember sitting in a coffee shop telling a friend two years later with the tears pouring down my face. Even now, nearly 10 years later, the old wounds are still there and it hurts to write about it.

Hannah's daughter stayed with her boyfriend for several years, during which Hannah struggled to come to terms with Mary's choice. They were lucky in many ways. The strong bonds of love which helped them to keep the lines of communication open prevented any major rift. Eventually Mary left her boyfriend and returned home. The story has a happy ending:

Both our girls have left home now, the elder married to a man of whom we are very fond and the younger sharing a flat with friends and working in London. We have a very good and loving relationship with both of them. My husband and I enjoy our life and home, welcoming daughters and son-in-law whenever they choose to be with us.

Although it was a very traumatic experience for us all, I believe I am a better person having lived through and learnt from it.

Sometimes a daughter turns on her mother for no discernible

reason, causing the most intense anguish. In a *First Person* piece
in the *Guardian* ('The Abandoned Granny', 1.7.92) a woman
wrote of her pain at being rejected by her 29-year-old daughter.
This happened without warning or precedent when her daughter
became pregnant with the writer's first grandchild. 'She hasn't
told me yet why she suddenly became so cold and even abusive,'
says this woman, and she is left to speculate, to wonder as all
mothers do, where she went wrong, and exactly what it is that her
daughter is blaming her for. There may not have been any specific
cause for blame. In some mother/daughter relationships the
struggle for individuation is a particularly fierce one.

Brenda spoke to me about her own feelings of pain at the
change in her relationship with her daughter who is now 45, a
child born fairly late to her mother and much wanted:

> I found the whole business of bringing her up an amazing
> *revelatory* experience. It opened up emotional areas in myself
> that I had no idea even existed. It was *magic*. She was a very
> easy child, quiet and intelligent, and I loved every minute. Had
> I been younger I would certainly have had one or two more
> but in those days 38+ was considered risky.
>
> We had a lovely, loving, harmonious life together – no
> teenage problems at all as she was a very reasonable child.
> Eventually she went to university. The house of course, seemed
> horribly empty but I found several agreeable hobbies with
> which to occupy my time along with friends old and new, and
> as I have always been a voracious reader, and my husband was
> home for lunch every day, filling in the time was not the
> problem. What I found distressing and so bewildering was the
> speed with which our beloved daughter distanced herself from
> us, not only physically but emotionally. She did come home
> quite regularly for a few days during university holidays and we
> of course visited her for the odd weekend, but it never seemed
> to occur to her how much we longed for the odd letter or
> phone call. I did not ask directly for this because I have always
> felt that if you have to ask for this sort of thing it is really not
> worth having, besides putting a strain on any sort of
> relationship. The times we did spend together were always

pleasant, but I felt that she wasn't really wholly there. She is, by temperament, rather self-contained and fiercely independent, so perhaps I should not have been so put out. She did once remark that she was puzzled to find that she was the only one amongst her circle of friends who was 'not engaged in a long-running battle with her parents'. There was really nothing for us to worry about as she was enjoying herself.

On graduation she moved around the country to different hospitals for experience and after taking her Fellowship she moved to London. In due course she married, which for various reasons involved a lot of pain for all of us, but that is another story altogether.

I don't think it would have helped at all if I had been working or even if I had another child. I sometimes think that a lot of what I felt (rejection, and a sort of bereavement) was perhaps because I put more concentrated thought, more effort and more truly loving care into mothering than into anything before and I think, subconsciously, I expected a lifelong pay-out on the investment.

Well, I *can* say that I had 18 years of great joy, and I try to comfort myself with this thought when I am hurt and almost frightened by the occasional cutting remark or response I get from the woman who *looks* something like my wonderful daughter, but is otherwise almost unrecognizable.

Are there clues in Brenda's story? She herself recognizes and admits the degree of investment she had in her daughter and her possible subconscious desire for a return on that investment. There is also the matter of a 'reasonable' child who had no teenage problems, who was the only one in her university circle not engaged in battle with her parents. It is possible that rebellion has come late; this is not unknown, nor even particularly unusual.

That wise psychologist, Dorothy Rowe, replying to 'The Abandoned Granny' article (*see p.156*) states that:

'Mothers have always provoked rage and resentment in their adult daughters, while the adult daughters have always provoked anguish and guilt in their mothers.' (The *Guardian*, 14.7.92)

I suspect most of us have been there. We probably all know women with apparently ideal relationships with their recently grown-up daughters, but they are not necessarily to be envied. The battle for self-assertion has to come sooner or later, and as these previous two stories show, when it comes later, it is infinitely more painful. In *The Motherline* Naomi Ruth Lowinsky says that daughters do not usually cut themselves off from their mothers in adulthood but:

> Ongoing connection does not mean peace and harmony. Many women have painful and volatile relationships with their mothers and daughters. As I have thought about the women I know, the image of wrestling has emerged to describe the differentiation process. In my image each woman stands on her own two feet, fully engaged in a struggle about identity, territory and power. When the dialogue of development heats up in adolescence and young adulthood, it turns into a wrestling match for renegotiating an intimate relationship.

Because we are made biologically in the same image, it is vital that we recognize our daughters' need for their individuality and that we treat it with the utmost respect. They need our unconditional affirmation of their developing womanhood and they need to be confident that we will not use our power – which is undoubtedly greater than theirs at this stage – to try to shape and mould them. And because this can be such an unconscious process, we should be alert for messages we receive from our daughters, spoken and non-verbal.

I have made the mother/daughter relationship sound like a battleground because it can be fraught with danger. But, along with all the women I know with daughters, I have found that the relationship creates an inexpressibly deep and wonderful bond, a connection at the deepest level of womanhood.

The Possessive Mother

Similar conflicts for similar reasons can occur in the father/son relationship but that is not within the scope of this book. The mother/son relationship, though, is another matter. I do not want to make generalizations and say that boys are easier, though many of the women I spoke to said they thought they were, but undoubtedly the relationship is less complex because in no way are there elements of comparison or competition. Even as I write this, though I can think of at least two young men who have stormy and far from simple relationships with their mothers, so I am very wary about generalizing. However, it is true that we do not identify with our sons in that same biological and emotional way and this gives them more freedom to develop apart from us.

But there is another type of intensity; the identification with a son as someone akin to a partner – a kind of emotional incest. The woman who experiences this will not be aware of its implications; what she *will* know is that she loves her child with a passion and does not want to let him go.

Sheila has a son in France, a married daughter living nearby and seems content with her relationship with both of them. However, she is desperately unhappy:

> My youngest child is 30 now and he is tearing me apart. He was always the most loving and the one I loved most and still do. I seem to have an intense feeling of loneliness now that he not only has flown the nest but also the country. He emigrated to New Zealand just over a year ago and he and his wife are expecting their first child. Sometimes my feeling of loneliness is so great that I feel there is no point in going on. I have photos of him in every room and I carry some as well. I pray every day that he will realize how much he misses us and come back home. I know I'm being selfish as their life out there is far superior to anything they had in this country.
>
> I feel that all the years of struggling and worry to bring him up have been wasted as just when I need his love he's not there. I would emigrate if I could but would not be accepted there due to ill health. I have a very loving husband who would do

anything for me and is very patient with my moods of despair.

Neither my son nor the other children know of my feelings of despair. I could not tell them because if John knew it would upset him and he would not settle, so my feelings are kept between my husband and myself. Whilst writing this letter I had to phone him just to hear his voice. Perhaps time will heal, who knows? Only God.

Sheila is not so much a possessive mother – if she were, she would not spare her son's feelings in the way she does – she is, rather, a mother who has over-invested her love and her self into this beloved son who represents all she believes can make her happy. She is wrapped in a cloak of impenetrable sadness; one gets the feeling that nothing and no one can reach her – not her other children nor her loving husband. She is literally living for her youngest son but he is the other side of the world and unlikely to return in the foreseeable future. Perhaps the saddest part of this letter are her words: 'I feel that all the years of struggling and worry to bring him up have been wasted, as just when I need his love he's not there.'

The hard fact is that we have children in order to lose them in one way or another. They owe us nothing. I have included Sheila's letter here as much because of that one sentence as any other part of it because of the implications it contains; that if we give to and love our children, they *owe it to us to love us back*. This is the root belief of the possessive mother; that her children are obligated to her.

Novelist Alice Thomas Ellis, who knows more than most about love and loss has this to say about the love of children:

It is very dangerous to have a child simply because you want somebody to love you because that's not what it's about. You love them and with any luck they love you back but that's not what they're for. They are meant to pass that on, they're meant to go on and love somebody else who will love somebody else – lots of other people in the meantime – but it should be a progressive thing. It's not reciprocal, not totally reciprocal.

Jeannie, married to Ryan for 15 happy years, practically exploded with frustration as she told me about her mother-in-law:

> She is *completely* unable to come to terms with the fact that her son, my husband, has left home. She has never forgiven me for 'taking Ryan away from her' as she puts it. She didn't have an easy time. She left home at 15 and had to live with an older sister, she married but her husband and all her children were killed in the blitz in the Second World War. She remarried at the end of the war and Ryan was born a few years later. She has no friends or interests, refuses to socialize with neighbours and only very reluctantly visits her sister and brother. She comes to visit us and criticises everything – the food, tablecloth, cutlery, TV programmes, the children's books and clothes. I feel that I cannot please her in any way, all my gifts are thrown out or given away to other relatives.
>
> She was seriously ill last year, so I take her to hospital for check-ups and tests but receive no thanks, even though I may have to take unpaid leave or arrange for a friend to take and meet my children to and from school. I wash her laundry every week and also do her shopping but all I do is wrong – wrong prices, wrong size of item, wrong label, wrong type of teabag, biscuit, cheese.
>
> I really am getting to the end of my patience and dread Christmas as she moans and complains all day – wrong presents, wrong food, – then wants to be taken home in the middle of the family film or game. My husband obeys her orders immediately.
>
> Recently she had a dizzy spell one morning as a result of not eating at all the previous day. She rang our number several times but every time I answered it she rang off and wouldn't speak until Ryan answered the phone. He then rushed round to her flat, called the doctor and stayed all day until she went to bed.

Poor Jeannie. Why not take a stand against this dreadful old woman, you might ask. Because, as in most possessive mother relationships, the son Ryan is colluding with her appalling behaviour. He is putting her needs before his wife's – possibly out of a misplaced sense of guilt. He is her only child and feels an over-developed sense of obligation, thus keeping the bonds of this unhealthy relationship strong and enduring.

It's a bit of a cliché – the idea that no woman is good enough for our sons. But like most clichés it has its roots in a certain amount of truth. When our sons have girlfriends, especially serious, possibly permanent girlfriends, they are presenting us with rivals. It is not always an easy time but it is one of the most essential parts of the letting go process, a handing over from one woman to another with the understanding that this new, young woman now has first place in his life. If we are wise, we will set out to befriend her. If we are lucky, that will happen naturally.

Extraordinary tragedies can come about through possessive-ness – events almost beyond the scope of imagination. On 9 November 1994 an inquest heard how Mrs Brenda Turner killed herself because she could not bear the thought of her only son being married. She flew out to Singapore for his wedding and then ruined the occasion by telling his bride: 'You have made this the unhappiest day of my life. You have stolen my son from me and ruined my life. He never used to stand up to me before.' Mrs Turner tried to kill herself after the marriage ceremony by throwing herself off the hotel roof but was prevented by her husband. Five months later she took a fatal overdose. At the inquest, her son spoke of how she had turned from a loving parent into a spiteful one, and had told his new wife that she would never be part of their family as they were so close-knit.

Mrs Turner was clearly depressed to the point where the balance of her mind was very disturbed. Cases like this are rare, but they happen. I think it throws a fresh perspective on the normal exigencies of mother-child relationships, however fraught they may be at times, and puts the concept of letting go into a different perspective. Those of us who have children, who let them go and then build an ongoing, happy, adult relationship with them are truly lucky. But it needs working at – on both sides. We tend to think we have done our job as parents when our children reach the age of majority, but the richest part of the process, the parenting of adults, the negotiation of that equal relationship is only just beginning.

7 EMPTY NEST, EMPTY WOMB – THE MENOPAUSE

It seems a pity to have a built-in rite of passage and to dodge it, evade it, and pretend nothing has changed. That is to dodge and evade one's womanhood, to pretend one's like a man
The Space Crone by *Ursula LeGuin*

The trouble with empty nest syndrome is that it tends to coincide with menopause. There is an abundance of books on menopause – I have a row of them on my bookshelves. Some commend the properties of HRT, some speak out against it. Some see the menopause as a rite of passage, taking us from our child-bearing years to old age – the three stages of woman: maiden, mother and crone. Some women do not feel ready, at 50 or so, to enter the age of the crone. Many of these books are concerned with the diet and lifestyle of the menopausal woman, others with the life of the spirit. They all have something to offer but it should be borne in mind that the reason there is such diversity among these books is that the same diversity exists among each woman's individual experience of the menopause. Not everyone is as lucky as psychologist Dorothy Rowe, who wrote:

When I was 51 I passed through the menopause without so much as a hot flush. I was not being gallant or protecting my family or denying reality. I was simply getting on with my life when an event, which, apart from nine months when I was pregnant, had occurred every month since I was eleven, ceased to happen. I wasn't surprised. Menstruation had never caused

me any problems, so why should the menopause?
(Time on our Side: Growing in Wisdom, not Growing Old)

Dorothy Rowe says that she was so busy during that time that she did not have time for a hot flush. She does, though, have sympathy for those women who do suffer menopausal symptoms.

I believe that those who insist that the menopause can be a positive and symptom-free experience are over-simplifying the facts, in the same way that some writers and practitioners insist that pregnancy is the time when we feel at our fittest and most glowing and that childbirth can be a painless, orgasmic experience if we do it properly. I believe all these experiences depend both on our attitudes – being willing to accept whatever happens – and on positive action, taking all possible steps to make the experience as rewarding as we can.

Much depends on how you feel emotionally about the particular stage you are going through. My pregnancies, for instance, were, by objective judgement, pretty terrible. I was very sick through all of them and had major complications with three out of the four. But I loved being pregnant with a passion because it was tangible evidence that I was going to have a longed-for baby, and because the excitement and wonder of the changes in my body and the growing, developing human being inside me far outweighed the inconveniences. Yet I accepted that not every woman feels like this, and that for some, much as they wanted their babies, the experience of pregnancy was nightmarish. The way we feel about our bodies and their functions is intensely personal and individual and there is no case for generalizing.

I can't say I felt as positive about the menopause. I felt I was too young – 42 – and I resented the unpleasant physical symptoms and the feeling that my brain was turning to sponge and that my previous mental quickness seemed dulled.

I think the clue to having a *relatively* trouble-free menopause lies in acceptance and in having a battery of practical tools and strategies to deal with problems that might occur. The emotions accompanying the menopause are of paramount importance though, and they need to be addressed before a woman can move on to the notion of acceptance.

Just as the beginning of menstruation signals the burgeoning of woman's fertility, so menopause declares its end. The language describing menopause makes it sound arid – no longer is anything growing or ripening; instead the ovaries shrink and atrophy, any eggs that are still being produced are likely to be of poor quality – hence the high risk of abnormalities in babies born to woman around menopausal age. We shrivel and dry up, literally, as vaginal secretions diminish and sexual intercourse becomes painful, necessitating artificial lubricants.

For many women, these physical reminders that her fertile years are over signify a double loss. The children she has borne have grown up and her body makes it clear that she cannot have any more. And nature, never one to miss a trick, can be cruel at this time. Many a peri-menopausal woman (one who is still menstruating and ovulating, though less frequently) feels an overpowering urge to have a baby – the last fling of the ovaries. This happened to me when I was 40 and I can remember what an overwhelming, irrational, primitive, animal drive it was. For a time it consumed me. My children had not left home, so it was not connected to that, but rather to my instinctive sense of urgency, that I was a woman with the capacity to give birth and should do so before it was too late. The awareness of time running out, the feeling that soon I would never again be able to conceive was distressing, as we had decided for very good reasons not to have another child. So logic and reason had to fight instinct and longing. When the menopause was under way, the urge disappeared, demonstrating that it had been very much a biological drive.

Some women, of course, do give in to this urge and have one or even two more babies, a second family, before the menopause. Most of us, though, are constrained by health and other practical considerations.

When menstruation finally ceases, many women feel a sense of loss and sadness which may spring from several different sources. The cessation of fertility, while providing freedom from the necessity of contraception, can make some women feel that their mothering days are over, especially when it coincides with their grown up children leaving home. This may be irrational, and women who do not experience this as sadness may find it hard to understand, but emotions around this issue are not based in reason or logic.

Other women are particularly sensitive to the loss of their younger selves, perceiving that menopause will render them less attractive. They fear losing their sexuality and feel that they will become a forgotten and overlooked class of citizens, no longer real, active, positive women. This is not vanity – our society is not good at honouring the older woman, and the values of our culture are based on youth and good looks.

There is also the matter of hysterectomy. Menopausal women are prone to gynaecological hiccups – heavy bleeding, fibroids, prolapsed uterus. Hysterectomy is often the doctor's first choice but there is growing concern both here and in the USA about the number of unnecessary hysterectomies being performed. Women tend to have strong feelings about this operation, polarized feelings, for and against. Some find the prospect of losing their womb deeply, psychologically distressing. There are many reasons for this and they are valid ones. Some feel that the womb is the core of their femaleness, some that they do not want the source of their fertility cut out of them, even if they are not intending to, or cannot have any more children. And for many women, their womb is deeply bound up with their sexuality. Yet other women, and they are by no means rare, are more than happy to get rid of a troublesome uterus: in fact, I would say they are in the majority. Having had a hysterectomy recommended two years ago – and resisted it, I have had far more women say to me 'Go on – get rid of it, you'll feel so much better' than those who support my desire to keep it intact. The fact is that there are usually alternatives to hysterectomy and this is a situation where a second or third opinion should be sought. The exception is endometrial cancer, when hysterectomy is not only necessary but often entirely successful in eliminating the cancer completely.

However, a woman who needs a hysterectomy and is unhappy about it needs to grieve, as if for any other loss. She should allow herself to do this and not feel pressured by the vast number of people who will insist on telling her that it is the best thing that could happen, or who cannot understand her feelings. As with all losses, it is only by acknowledging and grieving that acceptance can be reached.

And so it is with the menopause. It is a time for women to treat themselves gently. The physical symptoms can make you feel rotten and if you are unlucky in this respect, it makes sense to be proactive about it. Investigate HRT – it has to be an individual choice and for some women it can be almost magical. But it does not suit every woman and if you have misgivings about it, it is not worth taking it. There are many practical alternatives – you can buy supplements from the chemist especially for menopause. I was rather sceptical about these until a doctor friend of mine mentioned that she took them and that they really did make a difference to her hot flushes and incapacitating night sweats.

Diet during menopause is very important and can make a great deal of difference to symptoms. If you are not on HRT you can obtain natural oestrogens – called phyto-oestrogens – from certain foods. The main ones are:

Soya beans and soya products: tofu, miso, tamari, soy sauce.
Fennel, celery and other green and yellow vegetables.
Rhubarb
Ginseng
Alfalfa
Anise, liquorice, linseed.

There are other seeds and herbs obtainable from health food shops but for a much more comprehensive nutritional analysis, read *Beat The Menopause Without HRT* by Maryon Stewart.

The menopause need not be a nightmare. When you have helped yourself in every practical way you can, you will feel more empowered to deal with any conflicting emotions about the loss of your fertility and the loss of your children's childhoods. Many women spoke to me about this double loss. This is Lucy's story:

I was one of those women who dreaded losing my periods – I thought that while I still had them I was still young enough to be reckoned with. A sort of power – the power to procreate. But my menopause started quite young – 45– my periods got scarce and to my horror I started to go grey. My mother had not gone grey until she was over 50 (though now I wonder if

she secretly dyed her hair). I bought a colour rinse and it hid
the grey but I felt a fake. I knew it was there.

My son had left home a couple of years before and my
daughter seemed quite content to stay at home. She had
decided not to go to university and had got a job locally. But
the year of the menopause and the greying hair, she decided
she was not being stretched enough and she applied to
university and got in. Suddenly, it seemed, it was late summer,
my hair was getting greyer under the dye and my daughter,
aged 23, would soon be leaving home for the first time. It was
a terrible summer. I had always liked the hot weather but the
hot flushes and sweats made it unbearable. I was depressed and
miserable because Jo was going and I would be alone for the
first time in my life. I didn't like the prospect. I could see that I
would remain alone too – I had been divorced for years but
always hoped I'd meet someone else to share my life with. Now
– well, with my hair, my horrible skin and awful things like a
dry vagina, I thought my sexuality had crumbled away, that I
was no longer a sexual being and no longer a mother. The
feeling of loss, both that my daughter was going and that I
could never have any more, was quite disproportionate to
reality.

October, when she went, was *awful*. I felt that everything
was over. I felt terrible emotionally and physically. I couldn't
take HRT because of a family history of breast cancer, but I
went along to the Well Woman Clinic just to see if they could
suggest anything. They ran a Natural Menopause Group which
saved my sanity. The practical tips are helpful, but far more
than that I feel a kinship, a sisterhood if you like, with other
women who are experiencing menopause – many of whom are
also going through the empty nest time as well. We have shared
so much, wept together, confided in each other all those
feelings that seem so silly until you realize you are not alone in
them. And I look at these women and they don't seem old, or
ugly or past it. They seem beautiful and glowing and sexy. It's
made me realize that I am moving into a new phase of my
womanhood – a strange, as yet unknown phase, but one which
I no longer dread. I *like* the grace of older women and I don't

mind being one. We're in this together, just like women who are pregnant, or have young children, tend to get together. There's a wonderful solidarity.

I've made a big decision – to stop dyeing my hair. It's about 50 per cent grey now and there is a woman in the group who has long, beautiful grey hair. It's thick and has a wonderful sheen and she is so elegant and dignified. It's such an effort to keep up with the dye, and to keep checking for grey roots. I think it was my mother's generation that passed onto us this conditioning that grey hair was to be avoided and I think we owe it to *our* daughters to reverse this ridiculous idea.

I miss my children, but I no longer grieve for the end of my fertility. All sorts of clichés spring to mind about autumn, and about a time of fallowness and then new shoots later on (in the form of grandchildren) but I'll try not to lapse into too much purple prose! It's how I see it though.

Menopause completes a circle which began at puberty with the onset of menstruation and continued with pregnancy, birth, breast-feeding and the resumption of menstruation. Just as all those other events were important markers and milestones in our lives as women, so menopause is equally significant. It is not the end – it is a completion of one cycle of our lives, that of our fertility. The space it leaves forms the place for a new kind of creativity.

8 COMING THROUGH: HEALING AND A BRAVE NEW WORLD

Your joy is your sorrow unmasked.

The deeper that sorrow carves into your being, the more joy you can contain.

When you are joyous, look deep into your heart and you shall find it is only that which has given you sorrow that is giving you joy.

When you are sorrowful, look again in your heart, and you shall see that in truth you are weeping for that which has been your delight. *The Prophet, Kahlil Gibran*

Even a journey of a thousand miles starts with a single step. *Chinese Proverb*

With the help of the prolific and searingly honest stories of the women who have contributed so very much to this book, I have tried to examine the nature of and the reasons for the pain of empty nest syndrome. Many of the stories I have told sound bleak, for those women were at the stage of recent loss, and they had not yet worked through the process of change, grieving and adjustment to reach the next phase of their lives. That they will do so is certain and in this part of the book I want to look at how this can come about. At the end of Chapter One I suggested that this phase of transition can feel like crossing a very rickety bridge over a deep abyss. Now, with the help of other women, those who have crossed, or who are in the middle of crossing that bridge, I want to explore the process of healing and growth, for what is certain is that women's lives after the ages of 40, 50, 60, and 70 have so much potential for richness and enjoyment, learning and development, happiness and fun. In addition, those of us who are mothers are fortunate in having stimulating relationships with adult children who have now become equals and friends – though sometimes the passage to that relationship is a stormy one.

In Chapter Five I wrote about the process of loss and grief in some detail because it is not until this is understood and internalized that it is possible to begin to move through and out of it. A very real recognition and acceptance of pain is the first step to healing it; for many women the acknowledgement that they were suffering from empty nest syndrome and that it was hurting was the beginning of the process. In her excellent book, *The Courage to Grieve*, Judy Tatelbaum says:

> It takes enormous courage to face pain directly and honestly, to sit in the midst of such uncomfortable feelings until we have expressed them and finished with them. It takes courage to be willing to experience fully the pain and anguish of grief and face feelings at the time rather than postponing them.

For many women, this kind of work will have painful resonances from the past. It is important to remember that when children leaving home proves to be such a watershed, when this time arouses grief that is apparently out of all proportion to the event, it is because old losses, old wounds, have echoed through us, largely unrecognized yet demanding to be dealt with, because unfinished business is extremely powerful. In particular, the woman who herself was never adequately mothered and who has found in her own children the giving and receiving of love that she lacked at such a crucial time in her development is likely to feel abandoned or rejected in a way that may overwhelm her, even while she will most likely be unconscious of the link.

As my therapist friend Ruth said:

> It's about facing the 'why?' – daring to get back to the root and allowing oneself to feel. It's about looking at the pain full on, not hiding your eyes behind your hand and peeping out, or trying to hold it off, because that just keeps it going. If you dare to suffer instead of being frightened of it, then curiously enough, as soon as you say 'alright', it is never half as bad as

you think it's going to be. It's the diving in bit that is so scary. Once you are in there, there is always support. Women at this stage of their lives are armed with a good deal of experience of how to comfort people, which they certainly had not got when they experienced the original hurt or deprivation. They had no defences then, but now they have within them untold resources with which to comfort themselves and parent themselves. I do believe that if you take life on you will always find what you need to deal with it, to get you through it, whereas if you don't take it on, then in the very effort to avoid pain you live in it – or I should say exist in it, day and night.

Look at the fear. It almost certainly is a fear, usually of losing something. It's very important to be prepared to stop running away. The emphasis is on daring not to get it right first time because that's another thing that makes people give up. Have faith in yourself. You can do it.

I discovered that an essential element in the process of recovery was the destruction of false hope. Hope can be a treacherous quality, keeping alive, as it does, a kind of false idea of how things might be as long as we don't lose sight of the possibilities; but this kind of hope is rooted in the wrong possibilities and often uncon- scious. It is misleading and inhibiting to recovery; it whispers that perhaps our children may come back, perhaps they will visit often, come back to live at home, not grow up. This kind of hope is first cousin to expectation. And while this hope exists we are suspended, waiting for its resolution, and we do not get on with the rest of our lives. After hope there is passivity, then acceptance which is active, not passive. Acceptance rises to meet the chal- lenge of loss and pain and in meeting it begins the process of transformation.

Acceptance is the bridge – the end of grieving and the begin- ning of healing. It brings the greatest feeling of relief; the sadness and pain are still there, but you no longer rail against them. When you meet the pain and say 'Yes' to it, it no longer has the power to destroy. Acceptance is not easy, and sometimes we can only achieve it by an act of will – by making ourselves willing to let go, by being open to the fact that our mourning may contain its own hidden agenda which can cause some people to remain stuck in that stage for years. To accept can feel uncomfortable; it means saying – if necessary out loud – that the person or situation we have lost is never going to return, that things never are going to be the same again. Somebody once said to me 'Don't say never – it destroys hope', but this is treacherous hope, the hope for something that not only is outside the realms of reality, but which inhibits our growth and rehabilitation.

For me, acceptance was recognizing that my elder daughter who lives in America may well be there permanently. For four years I had fretted, wondering when she might return to England, making her feel uncomfortable with my badly hidden longing for her to come back. Acceptance is about what *is*, not what might be if we only wish hard enough. In my daughter's fifth year abroad I finally accepted that she may never come back to England to live. With the sadness of that knowledge came a great peace. I stopped fighting it and now our relationship is better than it has ever been. Acceptance was also putting away my preconceived ideas about the way my younger daughter at university might divide her time. As she made deep and important connections with the group of friends she has there, she spent more and more time in Sussex and less at home in the holidays. Acceptance was exchanging 'When are you coming to see us?' for understanding that the pressure of work, and the importance of her peer group are more pressing at the moment than coming home. And again I have gained from this; we have frequent stimulating and loving telephone conversations and when she does come home it is a delight for us all.

Acceptance does bring an extraordinary feeling of calm and order to emotions that were chaotic. I cannot tell you how to accept, I can only say that a willingness to do so, to let go of the thing you want so much, that you fear so much to lose, gets you more than half way there. Don't be anxious if it takes time to happen, or if you feel you have reached acceptance only to find yourself railing against your situation again. You will get there. To use a worn, but appropriate cliché, it really does feel like coming into a safe harbour after being adrift on tempestuous seas.

I am writing this on the evening of my son's seventeenth birthday. Much has changed over the years; this is the first birthday he has celebrated with both his sisters absent and only us, his parents, to spend his day with. It has shown me that I have reached the place where I am able to accept that the others are not here. I do not long for it to be different any more. And yet I feel that the family is still connected in a very special and enduring way. My daughter phoned from America to wish her brother Happy Birthday. We chatted about what she was doing and she told me she had been offered a job and that she was applying for a work permit. Part of me had hoped that when she finished at college she would return to England, but acceptance has enabled me to be open to all possibilities. I found that my first reaction was interest in the job she has been offered, that of a nursery teacher in a school for handicapped children. I know she would be perfect for it and that these children would benefit from having her, and that she too would grow from doing such work. I realized that I am now able to integrate the fact that she may never again live in England and that we will go on seeing her only once a year. But I thought of the loving contact we have by phone and letters and realized that the essential bond between all of us is intact.

My younger daughter is coming home tonight. I have not seen her for nearly three months and she could not be here today because she has a Sunday job. She is catching an evening train after work and staying for the day tomorrow. She faces a long and tedious journey tonight after a hard day on her feet. She will arrive late and tired, and it would have been easier for her to come tomorrow morning, but today is her brother's birthday and it is today she wants to be with us. I am reassured these days that family ties are strong and intact. She will not be able to spend the forthcoming holidays at home because of her job and because she needs all her spare time to work in the university library. This is a very heavy academic year for her and she needs and deserves full support from me.

What has changed for me is that I now feel affirmed as a mother through the quality of the relationship with my children, with the love and closeness that clearly exists between us all. I do not need their frequent presence to convey this to me.

The above is my own interpretation and experience of acceptance, so I was glad to find while reading a book on pain and loss, a definition of acceptance by Dr Elisabeth Kübler-Ross:

> a feeling of victory, a feeling of peace, of serenity, of positive submission to things we cannot change.

I am reminded of the rather trite but nevertheless wise Serenity prayer: God grant me the serenity to accept the things I cannot change, the courage to change the things I can and the wisdom to know the difference.

In *Healing Grief* Barbara Ward describes the 'transition curve' of recovery, a concept developed by Barry Hopson and Mike Scally in their *Lifeskills* training programme. The curve depicts the dip in self-esteem that occurs between 'the loss of the old and the integration into a new reality'. Hopson and Scally have found this transition curve to be particularly useful in cases of loss other than death – redundancy, unemployment, disability. With its emphasis on facing change and growing through it, it is an appropriate model for the empty nest phase of transition.

The first three stages on the curve relate to the stages of grief already discussed; *immobilization* (shock, disbelief) *minimization* (denial) then *self-doubt/depression*. The lowest point on this first part of the curve, the part that deals with self-esteem, is *acceptance/letting go*. This indicates the beginning of acceptance which is the first step out of denial. This is a crucial point on the recovery curve; moving out of denial and accepting the reality of the loss begins the upward phase of the curve that leads to recovery. 'Recovery from grief' says Barbara Ward, 'involves developing a new identity that allows you to function in the world without the person or way of life you have lost.'

There are three stages to the upward curve, or the recovery phase. *Testing* is putting a toe into the waters of this new phase in life; trying out different ways of being and doing things. It helps at this point if you can accept that change has indeed occurred and that you are able to change with it. Many people have said to me that when their children left home, they joined an evening class, started voluntary work or a new job and that they don't feel any different, that they are still mourning for their children, and perhaps more importantly, they are longing for things to be as they were. These women have not found the substitution of an activity or a hobby helpful because they were not yet ready – they had not gone through the stages of grieving and learning to let go. Those that had completed their mourning found pleasure and stimulus in the trying out of new things, the acquiring of small new identities.

I discovered that I really enjoyed cooking. The family were rather rueful at this, having been brought up on good wholesome but plain fare. 'You wait till we go away,' they said, 'and then start cooking all these lovely meals' – but the nice part of this is that when they come home I really enjoy cooking them special meals and they certainly appreciate it!

The second phase is *The Search for Meaning* and is about building a new identity on a deeper level. Many women at this stage enter a spiritual phase of their life. There is an enormous hunger for meaning, and the rise in popularity of 'personal growth' books reflects this. It is as though, as we get older, we become more aware that life does have a purpose and that we want to discover this. There are all manner of routes to finding this for yourself. While much of us is tied up with raising children, we tend not to have the time or space for introspection. It was during this period that I decided to think about what being a Catholic meant to me and whether it was still at all significant; I reject so much of the doctrine that I wondered if I could call myself a Catholic at all. I discovered that for me, rail as I might against the Pope, the Church and its teachings, the Catholic church is undeniably my spiritual home. When I realized this, I did not need to question it further, nor seek to explain all the anomalies.

This need not necessarily be a spiritual process. The search for meaning is essentially a search for identity which may or may not include a spiritual or religious component. One woman I know, during this stage, recognized in herself a long-felt hunger for Australia. She had been born there, and had not seen her birth-place since the age of six months. She took a trip out there, and to everyone's great surprise decided to settle. She feels that she is more truly Australian than British and that she has gone home. Of course, she sees her children infrequently, but being in her true homeland seems to have enabled her to integrate that.

Nor need this phase involve major changes. For some time after my daughters left home, I felt that my life must seem incredibly dull to them. When they phoned I never seemed to have anything new to tell them. My career had not changed, home life seemed as predictable as it always had. Then I made a simple, but deliberate decision: to accept invitations. I am naturally rather reclusive – many writers are – and saying a regretful 'no' to people had become a way of life. My social life was restricted to seeing a few very close friends. I decided I was going to say 'yes' to every invitation within reason. I was much helped by my close friend, Carol, who kept reminding me about my resolve. She also created situations for me to meet people. I owe her a lot, it made an extraordinary difference to my life.

Although reluctant at first, I found myself thoroughly enjoying the company of other people and the diversity of the gatherings I was beginning to attend. I joined a women's organization and made some very good friends. The search for meaning, which comes upon many women at this age and stage of their lives, has a two-fold aspect. We need to look inwards more than at any other time, to be more introspective and reflective, to try to find out who and what we really are. It is a time when long-held thoughts and beliefs are often shed as the products of conditioning as we find out what we really believe and through that, who we really want to be. At the same time, it is important to look outwards, clear-eyed, at the world and what it has to offer; perhaps to make changes in the pattern of our everyday lives and relationships which through usage and habit may have gone stale. It is, in every way, a time for reassessment, for preparation for the next important stage of our lives.

Jean's letter illustrates how this can happen, even when things seem at their most bleak:

> I am 46 now and from having my children in my early twenties I devoted myself to their upbringing. It was an experience I wouldn't have missed for the world and I have no regrets on

that count. I enjoyed being a mother, having been an only child myself I loved having more of a family life than I had ever had as a child.

My daughter is very talented musically and at the age of 16 was offered a place at Chetham's School of Music in Manchester. My son who was 18 the same year, gained a place at university. Of course I was proud of them both, but nothing had prepared me for the way I felt when they left home within three weeks of each other. I felt I had been cheated of two years of my daughter's life – I had expected her to leave at 18, and at 16 I felt she was still 'my baby'. Although both of them were only an hour from home I felt as though I had lost them completely. At one stage I felt that I would never stop crying: when we took them back after a weekend at home I would cry all the way home. The house was too quiet and too tidy. I felt that my life was over and I was only 40!

On the other hand I thought it would be nice just to be a twosome again and have no ties. I expected our social life to improve and for my husband and myself to have time for each other. Here I was to be disappointed. My husband had become little more than a workaholic and spent a lot of time away from home. He didn't seem to share my feelings of loss and couldn't understand my sadness. Suffering also from 'female problems' I felt ill, alone and neglected. No one wanted to know. My parents told me I'd done the same to them, admittedly at 20, and friends hadn't reached that stage yet and could only see the advantages. The year after the children left was the worst of my life.

My husband and I had one row after another; I seriously contemplated leaving, though I knew I still loved him. Suicide often crossed my mind, more as a cry for help and finally I rang 'Relate'. My husband agreed to come for counselling, though he would never admit he was part of my problem. My counsellor advised me to develop a life of my own and recommended that my husband set some limits on his work. I didn't feel I wanted to do things on my own, but realized I was never going to get my husband to spend as much time with me as I'd like.

It was while recovering from a hysterectomy that I had the time to do a lot of serious thinking about what I was going to do with the rest of my life. I began to feel better than I had for years with far more energy, so I decided to do something I'd thought about for years – go to university. My life has changed completely in four years and so have I. I went full-time to do a degree and gained a first-class degree last year. My confidence has increased dramatically. I don't think my husband has really accepted the 'new me' completely since I no longer do everything he wants me to, but we are happier than we have been for years.

As for the children – well, my son is living with his girlfriend and my daughter is still away from home but they both ring and visit us often and we all get on well together. Life has changed a lot. I still feel sad sometimes when I think how quickly the years have gone, but two little verses have given me comfort. I don't know who wrote them but they are very true:

> If you love something, set it free.
> If it is yours it will come back to you.
> If it doesn't, it was not yours in the first place.

> This can be our finest hour –
> To let go when we want to hold on
> Requires utmost generosity and love.
> Parents have to be capable of such painful greatness.

I was given an anthology of poetry by Dorothy Stokes and the title caught my attention immediately: *Who Is This Woman Anyway?* I wrote to Dorothy Stokes and discovered a woman who knew what it was like to embark upon a search for meaning. Four years ago, Dot suffered a crisis in her life. Problems crowded in on her and she found herself struggling with family difficulties as well as helping her husband with his business. She is diabetic and as a result of the stress, her diabetes went out of control, and so, she said, did her life. Suffering from nervous exhaustion, she knew she had to find a better way. She discovered a talent for writing poetry and this threw things into perspective; she realized that now she had something which was hers, something that gave

her an identity and a sense of purpose. The title poem illustrates
this:

Who Is This Woman Anyway?

Who is this woman anyway?
It seems like only yesterday she was just a child,
running through meadows of happiness and plucking at the occasional
    flower of achievement.
Responsibility and hard work were unknown growths of the future.
Life follows its natural progression – education, work, marriage, family,
    all very rewarding in an effortless way.
Effortless because the way is clear, one
era follows another
and she does not stop and say which way next.
The typing is there – do it, the beds are there, make them,
the baby is born, feed it, the children have to be driven to school, take
    them and always the job is there – do it.

Cooking, washing, caring, loving, minding, sacrificing,
working, cooking, washing, caring – CRASH.

Who is this woman anyway?
She did what she thought she had to do and so what now?
Children's independence leaves a gaping hole and busy husband so
    successful relaxes in attainment of that goal.
The woman looks around and sees deserted pathways
Plucks at flowers which daily die away.
Is this the time for sowing of new seeds?
Flowers flourish and die, but given their season
They must come again.
This is not the death of woman, but a new beginning
and daily she must nurture the dying seed within her to grow again.
Now is the time for dead-heading and pruning to the stem
For when the new buds come and blossom forth
There will be a show that nature has not seen before.

Dot Stokes' anthology plots her search for meaning, starting with
the question in the title poem and moving through an assessment
and appraisal of her life to a conclusion which shows that she has
found what she calls 'a better balance'. Now she is a deeply
contented woman whose life has an equilibrium and a satisfying

rhythm. She has found a place for herself. Interestingly, the crisis that precipitated her re-evaluation took place before her children left home and when her daughter went off to university, she felt she coped much better than she would otherwise have done. Her illness and breakdown followed the classic pattern of loss: she says 'I found out the hard way what it feels like to have that "gaping hole". It took me at least a year to sort it all out, but it may help others to know that women need to work out their lives for *themselves* and to have a real purpose in life'.

This can be a reflective time. My friend, Helen Kendall, coping with severe illness and other losses, found herself identifying with the upheaval in the landscape near her home; for her the destruction, the change and the chaos resonated with what had happened in her own life. The metaphor helped her to make sense of things:

On a hillside, near where I live in Bath, a new major highway is being built. With the destruction of thousands of trees, the movement of tons of earth, shrubs, wild flowers, insects and other creatures buried or burnt, homes demolished, re-shaped to create hard-core beneath a Tarmac covering, the landscape will be changed for ever.

I have seen the landscape of my body altered by pregnancy. The first time as my abdomen rounded and filled I wondered what shape I would become and what connection there was between babies I saw in other people's prams and my belly. I was very young. The second time, more familiar, I knew the world would change shape, re-shaped with this form. I understood my invisible underside though I could not see it.

Women watch. Some of us know pain, bear pain, understand pain. We did not think this road would happen. We grew our children and they matured us. We let them go because, though their faces still arrive from time to time and shade the landscape with familiar shapes, they no longer belong at home. Bringing up my children there was destruction, reconstruction, our worlds together reworked to fit us all. Marriage ended, home lost, fathers away. Tempers shouted, anger flung, tears dropped. There was pain. Illness wrought adolescent years,

death fashioned future, without grandfathers, without a
grandmother. There was ease. Arms extended around
shoulders. There was laughter. Bubbling in the chest. There is
love. Patterns on the ceiling changing colour. There is
happiness. Warm footprints on wooden floors. There is joy.
There is memory. There is landscape.

Four years since they left, some traces no longer remain. The
daily contact between parent and child no longer an aching
absence waiting to be filled. Photographs of men, once two
babies, fill spaces on the shelf. They lead other lives in which I
have no constant impact, make no constant response. In my
daily life they always occupy a part of my mind but cannot
figure in my countryside in the way they once did. At first the
gap yawned open-wide, painful and distressed. I wanted
comfort, to fill the emptiness in the way a breast will still a
wriggling, crying child. Now I emerge in a new situation and
once more enthusiastically knit my patternless life.

My mother was dead by the time I was the age of my older
son. What do parents of adult children do? I asked a friend,
bewildered by the status I had acquired by absence. Grown-up
children mean I'm in the age-range identified as middle-aged
and once more, just as the very young mother of a tiny baby, I
experience disquiet, belonging to a group I wasn't aware I'd
paid the subscription to join. And this new group has no
obvious badge. This time I don't go to the post office laden
with letters, a child in a pram and a look of newness that is
echoed in the face of the child.

When my children left home I wanted to adopt a distinctive
appearance that would signal to others in the same situation so,
like new mothers, we could recognize one another in the street
and take comfort from that recognition. Of course, just like
being a new mother, when I meet another we may discover our
common state does not necessarily mean we share much else.

Very little help was available from my parents but others
stood by offering their experience as a reference, their tools as
my equipment, their support. I was very fortunate. I found
another family who absorbed me like kin and lent me and my
children sight of their landscape.

As I write now the trees have been felled. For a time 20 or so remained harbouring the tribe who still determined to stop the destruction because they understood how slowly we can accommodate the changes we foist upon the earth. As my children grew my landscape changed slowly, at a pace we all created. Sometimes they pushed me into unwilling adulthood, sometimes I pulled them out of rightful childhood and sometimes, gladly, we have moved in unison, all at our own speeds.

Now I sorrow at the loss of the hillside and I miss my children. My views have altered, my horizons vary. Broad skies light into my room. Trees darken the scene. Stars shape and form the geometry. Hedges dissect and divide. Plateaus ease and lull. Vales dip and rest. My landscape has changed.

Integration

The final stage in the transition curve is *integration*. This is where the person, or situation that has been lost becomes, not a painfully separate entity, but an integral part of the experience. In the case of bereavement, the integration takes the form of internalizing the dead person so that the beloved becomes a part of you. Barbara Ward describes how this happened to her three months after the death of her husband. She was on her way to a job interview in which she had to make a short speech. She felt very nervous about this and on the train she saw an unusual building and decided to talk about architecture. Her husband had been an architect and she felt that he was talking through her. Over the years, she says, she has felt guided by him when she has had to make important decisions.

This does not apply in the same way to the change and adjustment we face when children leave home, but the principle still holds. I asked several women what they understood by the term 'integration' in this context. Some were puzzled, some attempted to express what it meant to them and some felt clear about its meaning, though it is not easy to verbalize. I felt Joan, whose grieving process was deep and long, and who now leads a happy, whole and fulfilling life, explained it well:

When my children were growing up, I was conscious of having several 'selves'. They even had different names – Joan, Joanie, darling, Mrs Langford, Nurse – and of course Mum. During those years, some of those labels changed; my mother, who called me Joanie, died; I went from hospital to work in a doctors' practice where I was not called Nurse. It was particularly hard not being 'Joanie' any more because I lost my connection with my childhood – that name had the ability to take me back, to hear my mother's voice calling me when I was very small. I grieved for her and I passed through the grieving, and eventually I stopped missing 'Joanie'. My children – one boy, one girl – left home within two years of each other and I was left with a great, gaping hole. I was no longer Mum. In spite of having all those other roles, that gaping hole sat there, huge, in the middle of my life, and my other selves just seemed to be at the periphery, almost out of sight. 'Mum' had gone. Yet of course, I knew I was still Mum. The children rang up and said, 'Mum, I've done this or that' – but they were independent. 'Mum' had taken on a different meaning. When they were at home, it had meant that I was at the centre of their lives – they needed me, they depended on me, they relied on me. I cooked for them, advised them about their options at school, helped them with career decisions, tried to help and be there for them when they were unhappy, when their relationships went wrong. Then suddenly, it seemed, they were doing all these things and more by themselves. I felt I was not needed and I felt as redundant as anyone given their cards. It was as though my role as mother had ended. I still knew who I was – wife, nurse, friend, etc. I still had clearly defined roles there. But I felt like a mother without children.

And that was the point of integration, if you like. Slowly I began to realize that I *was* a mother without children. I was the mother of adults. I still had a role, but it had changed and I had to change with it. I had to move from being Mum as I had always understood it to the Mum of grown-up children. It's a different relationship. It involves a lot of letting go and of accepting that they don't need you in the same way, and it is right that they don't. It means acknowledging their adulthood.

When I had done that I discovered that there was no gaping hole. I was still Mum – just a different kind of Mum, still needed and loved but in a different way. That identity is now as much a part of me as was the previous one, that of being mother to growing children. While I live and breathe I will always be 'Mum'. I am whole again.

It is not appropriate for me, or for anyone to impose a qualititative assessment on the depth and extent of women's empty nest feelings. For some there will be a constant, gnawing sadness, for others a feeling that life has lost its meaning and in between, a whole range of emotions. Any woman whose quality of life is negatively affected when her children leave home should be gentle with herself and look at the options; the wide range of helping aids or agencies that can take her through this time. There are things she can do for herself and there is the support she can call on from others. Many women, just beginning the healing process, talked to me about what they referred to as 'coping strategies'. They are individual, tailored to each woman, but they have all helped. Once you start to think in a positive way, you will find your own.

I found it enormously satisfying and healing to compile a *This is Your Life* book for my daughters' twenty-first birthdays. I bought a big red photograph album and started searching through all the childhood mementoes and records I had kept. I even found old diaries recording my first suspicions that I might be pregnant, followed by the joyful confirmation of the news and the children's births. I found I had kept their birth announcement cards and the congratulations cards sent to us; even the little name tag the hospital hung on their cribs. I had lists of their first words and phrases, drawings, old school books, notes to Father Christmas, their first swimming, cycling, music, dancing or sports certificates and of course, photographs, masses of photographs marking their milestones and important events in their lives. I left one blank page at the end for them to fill in with their own mementoes of their twenty-first birthdays. The finding, sorting, collating and arranging of the material took a long time, but it was immensely rewarding. It was also highly symbolic in a way that I had not expected, but which had meaning for me – it was as though I were handing over their lives to them.

I also marked the leaving of my first child by buying a picture in a Cornish Art Gallery. It seemed like serendipity that I went into that particular gallery at that time, the summer she was going. It is a print by Annie Williams called *Leaving Home*. Overflowing boxes and colourful carrier bags stand next to a homely kitchen table. There are books on a patterned rug and a teddy bear leans against one of the bags. It is poignant, signalling the moment of departure, the packing up of the old life, the anticipation of the new, with the teddy bear as the transitional object between the two. I love the picture. It hangs in my kitchen where I see it every day and it is a visible marker of a rite of passage not usually recognized as such.

Ann, still feeling bereft but determined to come through, made this list:

1 I don't listen to music stations on the radio at the moment because I will, no doubt, hear records that remind me of key times in the growth of my children.

2 I write down what I am feeling; hence this letter to you.

3 I look long and hard at the disabled young teenagers where I work and I see their dependence on their families, and I embrace the fact that for many of them there will never be the 'flight from the nest' and I thank God that my children are doing what they should be.

4 I do practical and constructive things for them (like baking their favourite cakes) and I focus on this as an investment for the future.

5 I plan long distance 'treats' for them that will lighten their load and help them. For instance, I send them a cheque so that they can go out for a meal, hair-do, cinema, etc.

These are my disciplines and they help me, most of the time, to cope.

Karen kept a record of her son's new life as a photographer on a cruise ship:

In the bleak months that followed (my son leaving home), I wrote frequent letters to him, and he in turn phoned us after every voyage. He told us such wonderful and inspiring stories that I decided to start a journal of his travels. I then kept a script of all his calls and filled my book with all sorts of souvenirs that he sent home, like air tickets, hotel bills, photos, vessel cruise schedules, even bar bills. Keeping a journal helped me to keep my sanity, especially as one month after my son left, my husband suffered a nervous breakdown and has not been able to work for several months. In July this year he was forced to take early retirement. Also my youngest son has had quite a few difficulties settling into his new school and has needed extra loving and attention.

And Barbara's letter illustrates how even the deepest feelings of loss can be transformed. This first part of her letter shows her at her lowest:

Last summer, not only did my son get a job in London, my daughter moved to New York for eight months as part of her degree course, and my husband moved out too during the week – after commuting daily for eight months we decided it would be better for him to find accommodation in Reading and come back home at weekends. So my nest was most certainly empty, to say the least.

I always just wanted to be a mum – I gave up my career in local government when Mark, now 23, was born. Gabrielle followed two years later and I was quite content to stay home looking after them and Alan. It was what I wanted to do. I felt it was very important, in order for Mark and Gabrielle to grow to be stable, secure, happy, adventurous adults that I be around to support and love them when they were children, and that going out to work just wasn't on. I did later get a job, a few hours a week, but it always had to fit in with the family – I wouldn't have been happy otherwise. And so life went on – never thinking of preparing myself for what would one day be my 'empty nest'.

Both Mark and Gay have indeed grown up to be

independent, adventurous, happy and stable adults, though this may well have happened even if I'd worked full-time or had a demanding career. It was my choice not to. I thought I'd get used to Mark wanting to 'fly' – when we moved from Derbyshire to Wales, he stayed behind with a friend for a year, to take his O-levels at his old school. He went to university after spending six months in India and after getting his degree at Oxford, he spent the rest of that summer trekking through India again. Fifteen months ago we went to help him settle into his new home, a bedsit in London in a family home. So why, when I saw he was so settled there and so happy, did it almost break my heart? Why did I feel as though I had been bereaved? I could cry now, just thinking about it. I felt like an animal wounded and just wanted to get back home where I could lick my wounds. I remember that train journey home. Tears were pouring down my face and I remember thinking over and over again how happy I should be because Mark was so settled and doing what he wanted, but I felt wretched.

Gay taking off for New York that same summer was not the first time she had left – she had already been in London for two years at college and I missed her like crazy. She's like me, chatty and I was missing her company so much. We both cried when we said goodbye at Heathrow, and I was hanging onto the fact that we would be going out to see her and that that would be wonderful. I'd always wanted to go to the States so the trip would be two fold, seeing Gay and New York.

But I ached when she returned in May this year and I watched her struggling to readjust from a busy exciting job in New York to a quiet time here with me before returning to college in the autumn. And when she announced that the firm she had worked for wanted her to return to New York when she obtains her degree next summer I felt so much pain, but I couldn't tell her.

And then Alan – how could I not miss someone who is such a pal as well as a husband? Who makes me laugh (and scream!) and always keeps me going when I feel down; someone I can rely on, someone I can moan to when I need to, someone I feel so happy being with. Someone I've loved for over 30 years.

So when they went I felt as though all I had worked to achieve had gone and that, even though I now have a job, there was no one to look after and fuss over on a daily basis. Almost as though I had been given early retirement at only 48 from the job I loved doing more than anything else.

A year after her nest had emptied, Barbara decided to make changes for herself:

I thought 'So what now?' A special friend of mine was at her wits end when a relationship ended and the advice I gave her was 'Never rely on someone else for your own happiness'. So I've decided I'm going to take my own advice. I'm going to make myself happy, do things I've never been able to do and I still intend to be close to my brood, but in a different way. I've always loved letter writing so as soon as Mark and Gay left for university I wrote to them weekly – sometimes a letter, sometimes a funny card I'd seen that had made me laugh, sometimes a strip cartoon out of the paper with a note. They probably think I'm nuts but it makes me happy sending them. If I'm stuck somewhere – last week it was in a garage waiting for my car to have an MOT – I write to one of them, last week it was Mark. I felt as though I'd had a really good chat with him by the time my car was ready.

I'm going to learn to play bridge. I'll probably be hopeless, my memory is awful, but it's something I want to do. London has always fascinated me but I've never ventured there alone. Two weeks ago I met Mark for lunch (actually used the underground from Paddington to Liverpool Street!) then spent the afternoon with Mark's girlfriend. I intend to go once a month, on my day off work, to see art galleries, a theatre matinée and the sights of London, knowing that if I get lost I can call either of my offspring to bail me out.

I'm interested in counselling so I'm seeking further information about it. I've always thought how frightening it must be to lose your hearing so maybe I will learn sign language and help some of those people.

I think I'm OK now. The pain has subsided and I'm

beginning to be able to spoil myself a little and to enjoy it. I try not to have preconceived ideas – and if spending the Christmas holidays with us turns out to be only Christmas Day and half of Boxing Day then I'll make the best of those times. And if there's a space, maybe I'll be able to arrange a game of bridge, arrange my next trip to London, or plan a spring weekend away with Alan.

Actually my nest is not completely empty. I still have Becky, our cat, and Nelly the dog. I talk to them constantly and make them listen when I'm feeling particularly grotty!

It may look as though I'm good at readjustment but it's taken me more than a year to get this far. And I'm hoping that by this time next year I'll have got even further. It's time now, I realize, to start to think about being my own person as well as a mum and a wife.

Such 'coping strategies' are not a denial or avoidance of the hurt, they are stepping stones, or steps across that rickety bridge to the next part of a woman's life.

The following is Jessica's story and shows how she worked to recover not just from the loss of her children but from illness which would have made many despair:

I have suffered from empty nest syndrome and come through it I hope. It was extra hard as I had suffered two mild strokes from which I was 90 per cent recovered and had also been diagnosed as having Multiple Sclerosis in a mild form.

I sat around for a while feeling sorry for myself and my friends drifted in less and less often. I hate clubs and the usual suggestions for lonely women so perhaps it was hard to find something to do. I had always been a busy woman with a business to run and after my first illness I was home all day and unable to do much. However, it didn't stop me putting on the kettle, so I used to sit in the window after breakfast and wave to everyone who lived on my street when they passed. I would lift my hand to imitate a cuppa and they would call on their way back. Step one – visitors. Step two came with the occasional baking of cakes or scones that they would like.

As the healing process went on and I was determined not to be housebound we moved to the country. I couldn't sit in the window any more and by then I had got back to driving and was more mobile. I had always wanted to learn to ride side-saddle so I made enquiries at a local stable and spent a wonderful summer out in the fresh air on a horse. It was much easier to ride side-saddle with my weak right leg, but with the onset of winter cold I couldn't continue. What now?

One day I accompanied a friend to the Record and Archives Office in the next town. When we were looking at all the papers I found a multitude of old documents about the village I lived in, and the people. I got copies and from then on I was hooked. I really gave the librarians at my local library a hard time but they never found a question too stupid or too small to help me find the answer.

I published a little book on the early history of the village and this led to the schoolmistress of the village school showing me the old Headmaster's diaries and before I knew it I had published another book, about the school this time, and then a third about the village in Victorian times. The last one introduced me to some fine old people who had lived for a long time in the village and I had endless cups of tea while they chatted about old times and supplied me with anecdotes. I made an awful lot of friends through all this.

I still do research and am now looking forward to doing a fourth book, based on the French prisoners held at this village in the Napoleonic wars.

There is a lot more! I go out to lectures and meetings. I catalogued books in a big old stately home and I found a job sewing in one of England's fine old country houses. This gave me the chance to work on the most beautiful laces, silks and tapestries, some 300 years old. That has finished now, but I now work in a smaller country house as a voluntary guide. Lastly I became a founder member of a new group which calls itself 'The Afternoon Tea Party'. Once every five or six weeks we put on a splendid old-fashioned afternoon tea with home-made goodies. Scones straight from the oven with home-made jam, cream cakes, jelly and cream and little cucumber sandwiches with the crusts cut off. We meet at four o'clock for one-and-a-half hours and indulge in this wonderful English tradition. We all get a chance to show off our cooking abilities and we can 'dish the dirt' in the true old-fashioned way.

I have three children, all married now, and three lovely granddaughters. I have always been available after my children left home, and I spent quite a lot of time making curtains and bits for their various homes when they moved away. Sadly my younger daughter went to live in Majorca and stayed for ten years with her husband. I missed her dreadfully but what a thrill when she arrived home eight-and-a-half months pregnant to get away from the heat, and had her baby in the nearby hospital.

My eldest daughter worked in London and now lives about ten miles away, and my son, having travelled extensively, has now returned.

No woman should feel that she is the be-all and end-all of her children's lives, but she should try and make them feel that help is at hand whenever it is required. It takes a certain amount of self-discipline to achieve this and sometimes I find myself slipping but I never want to become like my mother who always complained that I never went to see her and always made me feel guilty. I visited her every week for tea on a Sunday and often rang her for a chat but she very often used to sulk and put the phone down on me so I could never win.

Despite illnesses and family problems I have never been so totally at home with myself before. I am now in my late fifties and feel young at heart and so happy with my life. Most of all, I have a lovely family of whom I am very proud.

I found Jessica's letter inspirational – full of joy and energy and so strongly positive. She made up her mind that loneliness and disability were not going to defeat her and the result of her resolve speaks for itself.

A resolution like that makes a good starting point for a journey which will take us into a new and as yet, unfamiliar phase of our lives. How do we do it, though? I have been asked. How do we find our way there?

I have discussed the stages of grieving and of the process of assimilation and acceptance. Once it is understood that this is the essential stage of transition which leads to renewal, the work can begin. On a practical level, there are tools and aids to help us along the way; we do not have to go it alone.

Medication

In Chapter Five, I looked at the incidence of depression that can arise for women at this stage, often because it coincides with menopause and other family problems such as elderly or sick parents, and bereavements. If you think that your feelings/symptoms fit with the checklist for depression on *p.119* and your doctor prescribes an anti-depressant, think carefully about whether you want to take this or not, but be open-minded to the possibility. Anti-depressants are effective in removing the symptoms of depression and if you are holding down a job, for instance, you may feel you need something simply to help you carry on. If you *can* manage without medication it may be preferable because part of this healing process is facing the pain and going through it, finding out what it is about, where it is coming from and whether it masks other sources of grief. It is possible that anti-depressants may hinder this kind of work. They can, however, be a useful short-term crutch.

Therapy and Counselling

The empty nest is a life crisis for many women and if that is how it feels to you, you may find it helpful to be able to talk it over with someone who will be objective and understanding. Counselling, which may be available on the NHS at your doctor's practice, helps you to look at the problems you are facing and to work through your feelings surrounding these issues. It gives you the chance to express your feelings freely without fear of judgement and a wise counsellor will help you get a perspective on things. The counsellor does not change things for you, but helps you do that for yourself so that you do not remain stuck in the same place.

Therapy operates at a much deeper level and can last for months or even years. It is rarely available on the NHS though much depends on where you live. Therapy should not be confused with psychiatry, which is to do with mental health. Women at mid-life are increasingly deciding to go into therapy, and though many mock this as a typical American indulgence, a good therapist can enable you to discover parts of yourself you did not know existed and to understand aspects of yourself that have previously been a puzzle. A woman entering therapy with empty nest grief will find that the therapist will want to explore her childhood, for the process operates on the premise that the past provides the clues to the present. Often people seek therapy for one presenting problem and then embark on a journey in which they find all their feelings, actions, motives, behaviour falling into a comprehensible pattern, like the pieces of a jigsaw fitting together. Therapy cannot promise to cure your pain, but when you fully understand its cause, it is likely that you will be able to heal it yourself through understanding and acceptance.

Complementary Medicine

When you enter this field, you are faced with a bewildering choice of therapies. I once considered complementary medicine for a physical problem but ended up doing nothing because of the vast array of treatments recommended by friends, all of whom swore that theirs was *the* one. They suggested hypnotherapy, acupuncture, herbalism, past-life regression, cranial osteopathy . . . These are all fairly expensive and most people cannot afford to do the rounds finding the one that suits them. They probably all help to some degree, though whether the effect is a placebo one, I do not know. You're on your own here. You may be lucky and have a recommendation from someone whose judgement you really trust; if that is the case, I would say give it a try.

However, I do recommend two effective complementary therapies which won't bankrupt you and are worth trying. The homoeopathic remedies for grief and loss are *Ignatia* and *Natrum Muriaticum (nat. mur)*. These can be bought over the counter at pharmacists.

In a similar vein are the increasingly popular Bach Flower Remedies. They are tiny brown bottles with a dropper and you take a few drops of the essence, which is preserved in pure brandy. The relevant one here is Walnut, known as the 'link-breaker'. Dr Bach, who discovered the remedies, wrote:

> Walnut is the Remedy of advancing stages, teething, puberty, change of life. The Remedy for those who have decided to take a great step forward in life, to break old conventions, to leave old limits and restrictions and start on a new way. This often brings with it physical suffering because of the slight regrets, heart-breakings, at the severance of old ties, old associations, old thoughts. A great spell-breaker, both of things of the past commonly called heredity and circumstances of the present.

The Bach Flower Remedies are available from health food shops and some pharmacists. Both they and the homoeopathic remedies are completely safe and non-addictive.

Other Creative Therapies

Elsewhere in this book, I have observed how frequently women have told me that they cannot share their pain with anyone for fear of being dismissed, misunderstood, or told to pull themselves together. There is also the problem of the apparent conspiracy of cheerfulness – women telling other women how glad they are that their children are leaving home. Perhaps this is the time to 'come out', to tell your friends how you are feeling, to share this and give those in the same situation the chance to be honest, too. Coming through trauma, grief or sadness requires all the support you can get.

In searching for sources of support and comfort, we should not overlook the importance of the way we treat ourselves. We have been so busy being mothers, often sacrificing ourselves and our needs to our children, that we may have no notion of how to care for, or mother ourselves. This is the time to reflect on our successful mothering, to recognize that we have done a difficult job and done it well, for if we had not done it well, our children would not be out there in the world making their own lives. We need to be gentle with ourselves, not castigate ourselves for our feelings but have understanding and compassion in the way that we would if we were comforting someone else going through a difficult time. If we have practised acceptance, openness and letting go, we will be ready to move into an entirely new phase of our lives, one in which we are no longer defined as mothers, but as strong and able women with a great deal to give and a great deal to look forward to and explore.

I have learned many things through writing this book and I have made contact with a great number of wonderful women who have come to seem like friends, even though I have not met all of them. Near the beginning of my research, a woman called Helen Kendall contacted me and sent me a piece she had written three years before about her own empty nest feelings. Helen, like Jessica earlier in this chapter, represents for me the essence of what I believe coming through this experience to be. We have talked much about what our children leaving home has meant to us and I have learned much about Helen. I have been lucky for she lives in Bath, only 25 miles from me, and we have become great friends. Where there is loss, there is always gain. This is the original piece Helen sent me – a more recent piece of her writing, reflecting on the changing land-scape of her life, appears earlier on in this chapter.

Conkers lie embedded in their green prickly husks, waiting to be split, pierced, bathed in vinegar, then baked in the oven or subjected to ancient recipes to harden them. And to be threaded with string and hung between pairs of warriors who fight until one falls, unattached.

This winter they fill the carrier bags of other people's children, lie rotting in the corner of other children's bedrooms, roll under the cupboard in someone else's kitchen to block the vacuum cleaner in a hurried clean-up. My children have left home.

And with them have gone the telephone call at two o'clock in the morning to ask for a lift home because 'Andy didn't come after all, so of course he couldn't give me a lift home and you said I couldn't stay.'

Or the call at work to say, 'Nothing to worry about, Mrs. Kendall. He's had a slight accident in hockey, he looks a bit of a mess, but he's OK.' The nerve-racking drive to the school, fearful of what I will find, frustrated at having to leave work unfinished. The relief when I see him bloody, but still alive. The pleading to be allowed to borrow the car, money, have friends to stay when I am away, not to go in to school today (with the reassurance that no one will mind, if they notice at all).

I can now dispose of the 27 friendless socks carefully saved in the airing cupboard in the hope that one of my sons would reveal the hiding place of their partners. I can buy eggs, eat mushrooms, know the orange juice I opened this morning will last for the rest of the week instead of 25 minutes. I can buy one loaf of bread a week instead of two a day, and know most of it will be eaten rather than be scattered in crumbs around the breadboard, floor and table as if for the birds.

I can speak on the telephone without being asked where car keys, passport or cat food are. I can sit for a whole evening by the fire reading, without having to tell Rachel, Sarah, Miriam or Freya that he is out but wishes he were in to speak with her. Or that I'm sorry, I thought he was in but actually he doesn't seem to be. And Rachel, Sarah, Miriam and Freya know that I'm lying and that their heart's desire is standing three feet from me, tensely mouthing, 'I'm not in'.

I shudder at the rattle of the window frame, knowing it's only the wind bursting in and not the large forms of my sons – one returning slightly drunk from celebrations of victory in the local skittles team, the other crestfallen at the vagaries of a young woman's passion which has incomprehensibly receded overnight. And I no longer cajole, comfort, hold, tease, nag, sigh inwardly and smile outwardly, no longer dispense calm with inner panic, no longer speak with confident authority or quaking fear for their safety and health. I am no longer daily learning and understanding how to be a parent, no longer knitting my mistakes into the pattern of our lives together.

I turn to the photographs on the wall: one son smiling broadly at the camera, the other glancing sideways with tentative maturity etched around his mouth. Babies in bathtubs, children at birthday parties, five candles, six candles, nine candles, ten candles.

I drink tea from my favourite cup and think of the journeys, excitement and sorrows my sons will surely encounter. I pour myself a glass of wine at six and drink in the space and peace around me, and picture them growing from helpless babies to the men they are becoming. I relish my independence, knowing my sons are learning to understand their own. I eat my vegetable pie slowly and digest the times we have had together, the times when we are now apart and our future times together.

As I got to know Helen, I learned that she had suffered a devastating illness – cancer of the bowel – around the times when her sons were leaving home. She had two bouts of extremely serious illness, the second one necessitating her having a colostomy. She talked about the question of identity – a concept that appears frequently in this book and which is central to women at this stage of life. Helen had always defined herself as a mother and seen that as the primary source of her identity. When she became ill, she was effectively prevented from exploring her developing identity in the next phase of her life, because she then had a label – 'cancer patient'. 'It really is an identity you take on', she says. 'It is how people see you and how they relate to you – not Helen, the woman, but Helen the cancer sufferer.'

As Helen recovered, she found she was asking herself 'Who am I now?' No longer a mother in the active sense, no longer wearing the label 'cancer sufferer', the answer came from deep inside Helen. She discovered within herself an intense longing to write and a talent to do so. Her first two pieces of writing were accepted for a national newspaper, she has contributed a chapter to a book about living with disability and she has gained an MA in Creative Writing with a very promising novel in progress. She has used her experiences to start a popular series of classes on Writing and Recovery in which people explore, through writing, whatever it is they wish to recover from, whether physical, mental or emotional.

This has been the story of Helen's recovery – not just from her illness, but from the loss of her sons and her role as mother. There is no void in her life. She says:

> I'm learning to be someone else now. It was difficult for a time to know what that was but it has become clearer recently. I do see my identity as being a writer now. The process of separation, of understanding that my children are not part of me, was a very slow one, but you learn to become more detached. There's a kind of lightness – we aren't joined together any more. And I relish my independence.

Judith wrote to me about two years ago in a state of fairly hopeless depression. A single mother, with an only son, Judith was having a hard time coming to terms with his leaving:

> I left Toby's father years ago and have brought him up alone. I never found another partner – probably didn't even look properly. My main concern was that my son didn't suffer because I had decided to strike out on my own.
>
> I stayed in a job I disliked because it was secure. I took Toby on interesting holidays: Italy, Morocco, India, USA. I made sure he went on all the school trips, skiing, camping. He had music lessons, braces on his teeth, clothes, books and a dog, a bike – I was always trying to make sure he had the same as the other kids. I even provided him with people: keeping in touch with family, friends, acquaintances, more for his enrichment than for my own.
>
> When it became clear he was going to go, I didn't object. I was glad. I've never wanted to prevent him from growing up, growing away from me. I believe it is good and healthy and normal to do so. Why then do I sometimes roam the house, weeping?
>
> People keep saying things to me like 'Now Toby's gone you'll have all the time in the world . . .' And I can see it, all this time, stretching ahead of me like a dark cold tunnel.
>
> I don't want it. Why would I want to work, to read, to listen to music, if not to let it trickle down to my son and open up his

world? I taught this kid to walk and talk, to swim and ride a bike. It seems everything I did, I did in some way for him. Watched the News with him, went to museums, concerts with him. Bought a dog for him; I don't want the bloody thing now he's not here. I don't really want some of my friends; they were for him. There is a space in my head now which used to be occupied by my son and my concerns for him. He was the reason, it now seems, for everything. Everything I've done has been channelled through this now useless part of my brain.

He came home on vacation and after a few days said that he was 'homesick'. He missed his friends and his flat and his life up there. On one level I feel very glad, rather proud of him in fact. But on another, his words struck me with terror. I am shocked at the emptiness I have found inside me. Me, of all people, to be delaying doing his laundry because it smells of him. To be quite simply sitting doing nothing, staring into space, wondering what on earth I am going to do with all this time, with nobody to worry about and care about except a lonely old dog.

I'm bewildered and in pain and, sad to say, even if it gets better – and from what I've seen of other women it does – nothing will ever be the same again. I've lost those days forever. Strange sort of job, motherhood. If you do it well, you are made redundant.

I spoke with Judith several times during the following months and slowly she began to recover. Then she wrote me another letter, one which made me feel glad and hopeful and excited for her.

I have managed to draw a somewhat shaky line beneath those days I wrote to you about earlier. I am realizing, with amazement, that I had never thought ahead to the day when Toby would be grown-up. A lone parent of a lone child, I had focused upon him as my life's work-in-progress, obliterating everything else.

It follows that surely some of my grieving was for myself, marooned here in a job I can do well but don't like. I am also sure that much of the intensity of feelings is due to my own hard experiences of childhood. I could have gone one of two ways: been a distant mother, like my own, or embraced the task with joy, mothering both the child and myself at the same time.

I am amused to notice 'mothermode' keeps slipping back in disguise. Never one to take an interest in my garden, I can now be found upon my knees in the soil, nurturing seedlings. It's been healing for me to see what nature does. I cut back a buddleia, almost level with the soil. Spring came but nothing moved. It just seemed to lie there in shock, two bony branches protruding from the ground. I thought I'd killed it. But then life just seemed to break out of it, green points thrusting out everywhere, insisting upon another chance.

A good friend telephoned me a while back. Her five children are all grown and gone now and she listened with sympathy as I told her about my sorrow over Toby leaving. 'You probably don't realize it yet, Judith', she said, 'but at the moment you are standing in front of a wide open door. Go through it!' And indeed I have begun to see myself upon the threshold of something new. I'm beginning to get used to my son being away from home. I'm starting to shift position. That part of my brain which suddenly felt itself empty has busied itself making connections and now other images are forming.

One reason for this is the small piece of writing I did for you. More than just a simple catharsis, the very act helped me to join hands with my younger creative self and pull her through time to be with me. (I thought she was dead, like the buddleia.) Childless writers often say that their books are their babies, for me it was the other way about. All of my creativity went into raising my son.

Toby is in India at the moment. In fact, he has just telephoned from Delhi, full of hair-raising anecdotes. I don't ever want my loneliness, my neediness, my slow adjustment to his maturity to be a worry to him. It's not his problem. So it's clear, isn't it, that the last painful act we mothers must perform is to stand back from our children? We have to watch them whirl away from us into the exciting patterns of their own lives.

It's been a help to write about it and to know that I'm not on my own having a hard time over all this. Things are getting better.

I have noticed that a number of women have spoken of writing: how the act of writing about their feelings has freed something in them and moved them on a step. Judith found that she was able to make a great shift after she first wrote to me with her pain. Helen found that it gave her her identity. Other women involved with this book have kept journals or written short stories as well as writing detailed accounts of their feelings about this subject. There is something about writing that does free us – not necessarily commercial writing, or writing as a career, or even writing that novel you always wanted to – though I have always believed that the only thing necessary to write is the desire to do so. Journal writing is very creative and anyone can do it. It can take any form you like – a straightforward record of events and feelings, or it can be a collage of writings, drawings, cuttings pasted in, dreams noted, fantasies explored, diagrams depicting feelings, situations, relationships, symbols, colours. A journal is an original document and the more unrestricted you allow it to be, the more it will open your creative faculties. Writing helps us make sense of things – what is often a jumble inside the head takes form and clarity when it is written down. I recommend it for everyone.

Suzanne found that local evening classes actually included one on Creative Journal Writing. She decided to go along, having no idea what it entailed, but feeling instinctively that she wanted to create something:

> . . . more than a diary, not just a straightforward account of every day events. This was wonderful. The journal is more like a map of where I am, every aspect of my life. It's quite complicated – it's in different sections and some of them link with others but this is what is so marvellous – seeing it all written (and drawn) shows me which events, feelings, etc., in my life are connected – something I probably would not have seen had I not done this. And it is so helpful to look back, to read the journal of a month, two months ago and see that I really am on a journey of discovery, that I am changing and moving in new directions, thinking about and doing things that I would not have dreamed of before. I am quite addicted now to my journal – it's like a secret, private friend and mentor.

While reading an inspirational book about women's physical and emotional health, *Women's Bodies, Women's Wisdom* by Dr Christiane Northrup, I came upon the following meditation on motherhood by Nancy McBrine Sheehan, an American poet. I wrote to Nancy asking her permission to use her piece as I felt it expressed so well the core and meaning of this healing time. Nancy, too, is learning and growing through her writing: I felt it was another example of the creative process leading to transformation of the self. She gave her permission and I am happy to reproduce her meditation here:

Mothering Myself

In a society preoccupied with how best to raise a child
I'm finding a need to mesh what's best for my children with what's
    necessary for a well balanced mother.
I'm recognizing that ceaseless giving translates into giving yourself
    away.
And when you give yourself away, you're not a healthy mother and
    you're not a healthy self.

So now I'm learning to be a woman first and a mother second.
I'm learning to just experience my own emotions
Without robbing my children of their individual dignity by feeling their
    emotions too.
I'm learning that a healthy child will have his own set of emotions and
    characteristics that are his alone.
And very different from mine.
I'm learning the importance of honest exchanges of feelings because
    pretenses don't fool children,
They know their mother better than she knows herself.

I'm learning that no one overcomes her past unless she confronts it.
Otherwise her children will absorb exactly what she's attempting to
    overcome.
I'm learning that words of wisdom fall on deaf ears if my actions
    contradict my deeds.
Children tend to be better impersonators than listeners.

I'm learning that life was meant to be filled with as much sadness and
    pain as happiness and pleasure.

And allowing ourselves to feel everything life has to offer is an indicator
   of fulfilment.
I'm learning that fulfilment can't be attained through giving myself
   away
But through giving to myself and sharing with others.
I'm learning that the best way to teach my children to live a fulfilling life
   is not by sacrificing my life,
It's through living a fulfilling life myself.

I'm trying to teach my children that I have a lot to learn
Because I'm learning that letting go of them
Is the best way of holding on. *Nancy McBrine Sheehan*

The writings of Helen, Judith and Nancy provide the key to the
final act of acceptance and letting go. They illustrate that the most
important element in the process of developing ourselves as
women who are fully whole is our creativity. It is that female
creativity which we harnessed to give birth and to bring up our
children which will now enable us to develop our fullest potential.
Judith, in her garden, surprised at herself for taking an interest in
growing things, talks of herself as being in 'mothermode'. I think
it is rather that she has come through the worst of her pain and is
now in touch with her creative side. This is why she felt so
triumphant at the resurrection of the buddleia. At this stage of
our lives we have the best of all worlds. We have our children, and
the adult relationships we are forming with them, and we have a
vast reservoir of creativity waiting for us to explore. We are
inclined to think that we are at our most productive, our most
fruitful when we have given birth. Yet, after that, after raising children, there is still more waiting for us. Magazine editor, Janice
Bhend expresses this for all of us:

> Someone asked me once, just after my first son was born, what
> it felt like to be a mother, and I can remember replying that I
> felt complete, as if I had fulfilled my purpose. Now that I really
> have fulfilled my purpose and seen my children safely into
> adulthood I shall strive for that feeling of completion again.
> Many women feel, when their children leave home, that their
> reason for living has gone, that they are of no further use. But

once my nest is truly empty, I intend to make every effort to find myself again. Not just somebody's daughter, somebody's wife, somebody's mother, but a whole person who still has a lot of living to do, and a lot left to give.

The metaphor Judith's friend gave her about standing in front of a wide open door says it all. This *is* the moment to go through it. It is an exciting time, full of promise.

9 Finding the Woman Within the Mother

In the middle of the journey of my life I found myself in a dark wood where I could not find the way.

Dante, *Inferno*

After fifty, ageing can become an exciting new period; it is another country. Just as it's exciting to be an adolescent after having been a child, or to be a young adult after having been an adolescent. I like it. Gloria Steinem in *On Women Turning Fifty* by Cathleen Rountree.

The arrival at a crossroads is inevitable at this stage: there are choices and changes to make, for we may have a great deal of unoccupied time and space in our lives, literal and emotional. The two major life events of menopause and children leaving home bring us into what is now referred to as 'the third age'. Some women find this a difficult concept to accept because it is the beginning of our journey to old age and this is underscored by the loss of our fertility and of the mothering of children.

Much of this book has centred round the nature of identity. Women newly experiencing the empty nest often speak of uncertainty about their role – 'I no longer seem to know who I am' is a cry I have heard frequently. For a time, these women's sense of definition eludes them: they know with certainty who they have been until now but they cannot imagine who they will become. Letting go of the known and familiar stirs up apprehension yet there is so much that is possible, so much that is exciting. This is the age when women are free to find their identities without reference to anyone else.

When we are young, we are preoccupied with finding a partner, and to some extent, moulding ourselves into what that person would like us to be – this is part of the need to conform that besets women at a time when most are biologically driven to find a mate. Then, as we have seen, our identities become strongly defined in terms of motherhood. I am not talking here about the women who become *over*-identified with their children, but again, about a biological necessity that we relate to our children in this way when they are young.

Now it is time for *us*, and standing alone, without these badges of identity can be exhilarating, if we let it, and if we have experienced and completed the process of mourning and letting go of our old identities.

Stella Clark and Dot Stokes, both of whom produced anthologies of poetry from which I have quoted earlier in this book, have each written poems expressing this sense of discovery of their existence as women in their own right. These poems capture the essence of the realization that we do not exist in relation to others; that we have become truly ourselves and that it is time to go forward in this new autonomy. This is not to advocate selfishness or any kind of dissociation from our families, but it is an acknowledgment of the freedom we have gained, probably for the first time in our lives – the freedom to be who we truly are.

Cheese

In the recent few months I've decided
The image is getting quite clear
I've somehow got left out of the picture
It only clicked early this year.

You know, like those kind of bad photos
Where the heads get chopped off at the top
And unidentifiable bodies
Make the picture an almighty flop.

I've always been there in the background
The mother, the daughter, the wife
But when it comes down to sharp vision
There's no focus upon this great life.

'You must be so-and so's mother'
'That clever man's married to you?'
But as to your identity, really
They certainly haven't a clue

When surrounded by all sorts of talents
My family don't notice it seems
The shots and the pictures there waiting,
Don't look at my hopes and my dreams.

Well now is the time for a new film
There'll be some incredible prints
'Cos the place where they're aiming the camera
Is dropping some blooming great hints.

We'll bring out the zoom lens and use it
And take off the lens cap on life
Then they'll look at the frame in the future and say
'I didn't know she was your wife'. *Dot Stokes*

Labels

We acquire labels from the day of our birth,
As daughter, sister, friend, lover, maybe wife,
Perhaps mother, grandmother, who knows,
There's no shortage of labels for each stage of our life.
We become totally covered with labels,
So that our vision's obstructed, our speech is distorted,
Our movement restricted, and hearing impaired
By labels.

But if we take courage and refuse to be labelled
And painfully peel away others' perceptions,
What remains under that papier mache?
Someone who says
'Yes, I am all those things
And I give my love freely
But I hold my life dearly
And the label I choose now is
ME'. *Stella Clark*

This question of identity, perhaps more important now than at
any other time of our lives, is an endlessly fascinating one. It is so

much more than *doing* something, it is intimately connected with *being* someone. It is that person we have to look for deep within ourselves.

At a weekend retreat for women, I met Claudine, who told me of her lifelong struggle to find out who she really was, though she did not at the time realize that this was what she was doing. All she knew was that she was perpetually unhappy and could not seem to 'get it right'. Claudine is half French and identifies more with her French side. As a young woman she had felt a certain confidence because of her unusual and dramatic good looks. She had no shortage of admirers and attention but the confidence this gave her was spurious. She excelled at art and at 18 she went to art school in Paris. As expected, she did well and was tipped for a promising career but at art school things started to go wrong. She developed an eating disorder and other emotional problems and was often severely depressed. She found a 'rescuer' in the form of one of her tutors who fell in love with her. He asked her to marry him and the idea of such security was irresistible to Claudine, though she knew she was not in love with him. She married him, but dropped out of college a year before graduating.

Claudine had three children and devoted herself to their upbringing. Her marriage was not happy but she stuck at it. As her children got older and her husband more and more distant, she developed a strong sense of needing something to identify herself by. She started to paint again, frantically, obsessively and her unhappiness increased. She was beset by a double sense of failure – that she had not seen her studies through and graduated and that her painting, though perceived as good by objective critics, was not up to standard as far as she was concerned. Claudine actually hated painting by this time and felt a split in her personality. She was doing the thing for which she felt she had talent, but it was doing nothing for her and she could not understand why.

Her interior unhappiness and dissatisfaction was at odds with the way she was perceived by the outside world. Claudine was popular and admired. She had three bright children and a well-respected husband. She had one or two successful exhibitions which increased her social and professional standing. It made no difference. She felt, she said, that she was 'nobody' and still saw herself as a failure despite all evidence to the contrary.

As her eldest child approached school-leaving age, Claudine decided to make a clean break. She left her husband and her unhappy marriage and returned to England. When her two elder children were at university, she decided to go into therapy to try to find out what was blocking her and why she still felt such deep inner unhappiness and discontent. To her surprise, her therapist suggested that painting might not be the right thing for her and asked if there was another direction that Claudine felt she could move in. No, said Claudine, she had always been good at art, everyone had said she would paint, she had done well – if only she could get it *right*. If only she could feel some sense of fulfilment in her work, if only she could *identify* with it. After all these years, she found something alien in herself as a painter. Leave it for a bit, her therapist said; let it go and wait to see if anything fills the space. So Claudine stopped painting and was filled with a tremendous sense of freedom and release. She never again wanted to pick up a paintbrush, though this made her very anxious. Her children were grown-up. 'I thought – if I didn't paint,' she told me, 'then who would I be? Painting had driven me almost to the point of madness, but it was what I had always known and how I was judged – favourably – by the world. But I had to listen to my therapist because I realized that painting was sucking the life-blood out of me and had been doing so for years.'

Within this period of waiting, Claudine began to question her identity as a mother as well as a painter. Her third and last child left home and she felt as if she were in crisis. She had been secure in her role as a mother but with the loss of that, too, she felt entirely directionless. She told me, 'It was like being in a great black void, a dark tunnel. I couldn't see the light at the end of it, I couldn't see where I was going. I didn't know how to explain to people that I wasn't painting, and I was very tempted to start again because was something I *knew*.' But Claudine's therapist said 'Wait' and so she waited. A year passed, two years. She had time on her hands. She got a job, part-time, in a health food shop and cafe. She enjoyed it but knew it was only part of the waiting time. Meanwhile, in therapy, she was learning about herself, gaining insights into her earlier unhappiness, her eating disorder and her need for a father figure in the shape of the tutor she married.

Claudine realized, though she cannot remember at what stage, that not only was she gaining a great deal from her therapy, she was becoming increasingly fascinated by the process. She found herself analysing the ways in which her therapist found the route to hidden issues, how she helped Claudine to untangle knots without giving direct advice. She started going to lectures on psychology and gradually she came to know, with a certainty she had never before felt about anything, that this was what she wanted to do with her life. When her own therapy finished she went into training and she is now a qualified, practising psychotherapist. She is more than content, she is utterly at home within herself. It is, she says, as if she had always been out of place in her own life. And one unexpected offshoot – she has started painting again. Now she enjoys it, and her style has changed entirely, reflecting, she thinks, the person she was meant to be, rather than the person she was trying to be.

What I found fascinating about Claudine's story was that it demonstrates that who we become, when our vision is clear, when we are no longer distracted by putting others first, is not necessarily the same as what we have been. Finding the woman within the mother means unpeeling layers of conditioning and assumptions. With Claudine's talent and her success as a painter, it seemed clear that this was the key to who she was. In fact, it was what she *did*.

In Claudine's case the story was a fairly dramatic one because her 'mistaken identity' led to such unhappiness and confusion. It is, though, increasingly common for women at mid-life to change direction. We have the time to stand back and look at our lifestyles and we are often surprised at what we discover; that the career, or way of life that seemed to satisfy us until now, no longer does so. It is not that our particular choice was wrong in the first place – usually it was expedient or right for us at the time. But at this stage women often undergo a sea-change – the 'change of life' is not so named simply because we cease to menstruate. Our vision changes, *we* change. I believe that consciously, or unconsciously, we look back over our lives and find those parts of ourselves that we have never fulfilled. It is not always an easy transition into this new life. Claudine was not the only woman who spoke in terms of the darkness of that period. When our children have left home and we are moving into this new, uncharted stage of our lives, what we shall do in it may not be immediately apparent to us.

Sometimes there has to be a hiatus, a period of what feels like emptiness, a sense of 'What am I going to do with the rest of my life?' This is like the stillness of the dark earth in winter. Nothing moves but underneath there are seeds, bulbs, waiting for a new season. 'If you feel like this, stay with it,' said my therapist friend Ruth. 'Don't rush into activity just for the sake of doing something. Take time and listen until you hear within you what it is you are meant to do.' This feels right and probably explains why many women, who took up work or hobbies or joined organizations when their children left home, felt that these things did not help to fill the gap. They had precipitated themselves into displacement activity which filled their time but not their minds, or hearts or souls. We need to bear in mind that we are evolving and this is not an instant process.

Some women are fortunate. I think of Gillian, who completed her university degree and married and had children immediately afterwards. She stayed at home with her children for 18 years, content to be a full-time mother with the knowledge tucked away inside her that she had all her academic potential to fulfil when the time was right. When that time came, it was writing that drew Gillian. She became a successful freelance journalist and had a book published. She found deep spiritual needs within herself and became a convert to the Russian Orthodox Church, of which she is now the General Secretary for Britain. And she is lucky in her relationship with her husband which has become a central part of her life.

Gillian recognized the unfulfilled part of herself, even, she says, having a sense of guilt about the waste of her academic training. She knew that she would use it in time, but she did not know the form it would take. Her writing and her need for a deep spirituality coincided – her book is a collection of reflections on St.

Matthew's gospel. She has found her place in the new order of things: 'There's a lot of life out there waiting, and my time has come.'

Ellen is a woman I met when I was researching this book. She was working as a tax consultant and as I got to know her, I could not quite reconcile her profession with the vivacious, warm and creative woman who was fast becoming a friend. I knew she had built up a successful business and had warm relationships with her clients. One day she told me she hated her job and had discovered in the past year or so that she wanted to be a journalist. She had already had some pieces published in a minor trade magazine but wanted to change careers. I advised caution. Journalism, I told her, is a treacherous profession, unstable, unreliable and highly competitive. Ellen was fascinating. She had taken herself on an inner psychological and spiritual journey to find the woman within and had learned a great deal about why she had become the person she was. She had always wanted to please her parents, to earn their love and even in middle age she was locked in an ambivalent relationship with them in which they gave or withheld their love and approval according to their own whims. She realized that she had gone into tax to please her father – it had been his profession. Her tentative forays into writing displeased her parents and at first she could not understand why. She began to see clearly which aspects of her they approved of and which they rejected and realized that she had been dancing to that tune all her life. They approved of motherhood, so she was safe there. But she knew that to find the real Ellen she would have to go through the painful process of cutting herself off from them emotionally.

In the two years I have known her, I have witnessed phenomenal changes in Ellen. I have watched her grow in confidence and acquire a sense of herself that was previously absent. And despite my warnings, she has made it as a journalist, against all odds. She is now a regular contributor to a national daily newspaper and writes features for a weekly women's magazine – a pretty meteoric rise in this profession. Her parents do not acknowledge her success and this has been painful for Ellen. They never read what she writes and if she shows excitement or enthusiasm, she is told she should have stayed in tax. But Ellen has become the woman she was meant to be. I realized this when she told me she had gone out and bought herself an expensive Chanel handbag. The former Ellen would never have believed herself worth such a thing – all her giving was to the children and her parents. Everyone else had always come first.

I do not believe that we can find this dormant, unfulfilled part of ourselves while we have our children at home. Their leaving frees us and empowers us to make important discoveries about ourselves. This psychological journey to find the woman within the mother is an essential part of this change, though in many women it occurs gradually and spontaneously, often unconsciously. It does not have to be a deliberate search, such as Claudine and Ellen undertook.

Looking around at my 'third age' friends and colleagues, I realize how much we are all changing. I have just received a letter from the woman who was my best friend at school and who has become a close friend in adulthood. Her children are settled in jobs and she herself has worked full-time for many years. I remember at school being surprised that Celia did not go to university – I was sure she would. Her letter informed me joyfully that she had embarked on a degree course. 'I've always wished I had a degree,' she said. Celia has located that particular unfulfilled bit of herself and integrated it.

Not everyone embarks on degrees, of course, or changes their job, or starts training for a new profession, though 1 believe it is significant that a large number of women become restless at this stage in their professional lives and look within themselves to try to discover what it is they *really* want to be doing. For women in the nineties, the opportunities have never been so good. The range of university degrees and other higher education courses is so wide now that choices are exciting and there is a much greater receptiveness to mature students. There are opportunities for women returners to the workplace and for career changes. Women in their fifties are starting their own businesses for the first time, doing what they want to do, loving it and making a go of it. There is nothing to stop us.

The search for wholeness is, I believe, a primitive, instinctual thing which we embark on in order to become complete in ourselves before we die. Just as we have no rite of passage for the end of our time of active mothering, so there is no rite of passage for passing into this last third of our lives. We create it for ourselves without knowing we are doing so. As our relationships with our children change and move into a different place, so too do our relationships with others. This is a particularly significant time where friendships with other women are concerned. Several women have told me that they re-evaluated their friendships at this stage and found that they had outgrown certain people whom they considered friends more out of habit and familiarity than anything else. Friendships can be like marriage – you may rub along for years then realize one day that you no longer have anything to say to each other because you have both changed. What do you do? Surely you don't just drop your friends? Katherine wrote and told me how this was a part of the many changes she made in her life:

I knew, at 50, that it was time to change my life completely and radically. It was not an easy decision because it meant leaving my husband, which was painful but the right thing to do, and getting tough with my sons. In fact, I threw them out (making sure they had somewhere to live) because they would not get off their backsides and do something with their lives. Now they have both got jobs. I work full-time and earn a good salary so I bought myself a little cottage. I no longer wanted to be at all dependent on my husband. I realized that everything I had ever done, including marrying this man and training for my job, was because other people expected it of me. At the age of 50, I went through a very late rebellion! I hate my job – I am a nursing sister and used to love nursing but I can't stand the new system. It's all paperwork and I will get out, but I don't yet know what I am going to do. All these huge changes feel quite overwhelming and I get scared sometimes. What keeps me going is that I know that I am doing the right thing. I feel shaky and uncertain – but more me than I ever have before.

It feels as though I'm having a real spring-clean – but the other thing that has changed is my friendships. This sounds really calculated but when I had moved, I thought about my friends individually and decided quite deliberately to let some of them go out of my life. I had changed such a lot and I found that I just no longer connected with some of these women. We had had our good times, we'd had things in common, like work or bringing up children, but I'd outgrown them. My criterion was – if I met this person now, would we form a friendship and if the answer was no, then I ended the relationship. I knew other women who had felt the same about friendships – I guess it's not that uncommon, after all we do change as we get older. One or two people said they had just let things slide, stopped getting in touch or being available but I didn't feel that was honest. So I told them, in a letter if they were at a distance, or face to face if possible that I felt that our friendship had outgrown itself and that although I would always be fond of them, I felt we didn't have enough to share any more. It was quite painful but no one reacted adversely. I guess that if I was feeling that way the chances were that they were too and perhaps they were glad to have it out in the open. It sounds hard, but life is too short to focus on who, or what is not really important.

Then there was an awful time when I felt really adrift. I had left everything that had always been familiar and I had cut myself off from old friends. Then somebody said to me – 'It will be alright because whenever there is a space, something comes along to fill it', and I thought well, yes, nature abhors a vacuum! I joined women's groups and started some classes and of course I met people. And some of those people became friends, real friends, because we were recognizing in each other something greater than just having things in common. We have real rapport.

I suspect most of us would not have the courage to face our friends as honestly as Katherine did; mostly we just lose touch, however good our intentions. It is true that many of the friendships we form when we are younger come about through shared parenthood or other common bonds. I have lost touch with several of those friends but the friendships I have formed in the past few years are stronger than most. I have a few close friends who go way back and who are very special – a shared history is a strong bond.

The discovery of the importance of friendship is, I believe, another part of this journey. I am more conscious than at any other time in my life of how much my friends mean to me and what an infinitely precious thing real friendship is. I know that this awareness is shared by other women at this point in their lives. When our children have left home, we are less intensely focused on the family – we have room to give and receive more from other relationships. In *Ourselves Growing Older*, the authors comment that:

> For all of us, irrespective of marital status or sexual preference, women friends provide the support and continuity that enable us to enjoy new challenges and cope with the changes and losses we face in the second half of life. With this awareness, growing numbers of us are learning to regard our friendships as lifelong relationships to be worked at and cared for 'just like family'.

As we discover more of this woman within, we may find ourselves becoming more spiritual and philosophical. By this I do not necessarily mean religious, though this may be part of the process for some of us. Again, I believe this to be an instinctual thing. We have experienced the material, intellectual and emotional aspects of life, and though many women will have incorporated a religious or spiritual component, it is common at this stage to question and to seek further. In Chapter Five I explained how I came to query and to re-evaluate Catholicism. It makes sense – both to take a fresh look at something familiar and perhaps jaded, and to explore new pathways. Some women have insisted to me that they do not need a spiritual element in their lives. I would challenge this simply because we are all made up of the physical, mental, emotional and spiritual. We cannot leave out one aspect of ourselves if we are seeking wholeness. Spirituality does not have to follow a recognized path. It can mean whatever we want it to mean; it is entirely personal.

The power of the changes that can take place at this stage of our

lives was demonstrated to me by my friend Caroline. She was a
strict and devout Catholic who believed implicitly in the Church's
teachings on everything. She never missed Mass or Confession.
No one ever discussed Catholicism with Caroline because for her
it was a given. There was nothing to discuss. She moved away
from the area just after the last of her children had left home and I
did not see her for about two years. We met for lunch recently
when she was back on business. During our catching-up conversation she told me she had left the Church. It was like hearing that
Margaret Thatcher had deserted the Tory party – the shock/
surprise value of the announcement carried the same impact.
Something – Caroline did not know what, it was non-specific –
had made her start thinking hard about the Church and slowly, it
had dawned on her that she did not actually believe any of it. It
was received teaching, conditioning, indoctrination and had been
part of her life since childhood, and therefore, she thought, an
integral part of her. She was not even sure whether she believed in
God. Since her enlightenment, she had been reading widely, all
manner of spiritual texts from Buddhism to New Age and was
acquiring a sort of eclectic spirituality with no main focus. Never
again, she said, would she have anything to do with organized
religion. She believed it to be a form of oppression, a subduing of
people's will and autonomy.

You would have to know Caroline to appreciate the enormity of
this *volte face*. She was one of those people whose religion made
her appear too good to be true. She *was* too good to be true – she
was not real. But now she has stripped the layers of imposed belief
and behaviour and is becoming her true self. The abandoning of
her meek, unquestioning obedience to the Church has caused her
to look for other truths in other aspects of life. She would not
have thought about any of this when her children were still at
home, for she had brought them up in the faith and sent them out
into the world hoping that faith was intact.

I see these changes gradually taking place in myself and in my
friends and I find it exciting. There is so much to discover and at
this age we now have the confidence to change without feeling
we have to please somebody else. And this process brings us closer
to our children – they need us to be ourselves and they approve of

us striking out in new directions, just as they are doing. Gillian told me about an impetuous backpacking trip she and her husband made through South America. Only when they were deep in a jungle did they realize that nobody knew where they were. 'I think the children are secretly amazed at suddenly finding themselves with delinquent parents,' she said. 'But they respect us. And, you know, I think they're a trifle envious. At their time of life the world can be a pretty serious place.'

Fifty and Beyond

The fiftieth birthday is a significant one for both sexes – the realization that we have lived for half a century is fairly awesome. It is also a kind of 'halfway mark' – with life expectancy for women greatly increased there are a good number of nonagenarians around. But 50 also brings to mind our mortality and makes us realize with what alarming speed our lives have passed. Women at 50 have measurable, identifiable evidence of having reached this age, whereas men remain unchanged, apart from greying hair and a spreading waistline. As every woman knows, there are double standards operating here – my husband's grey hair is admired as being 'distinguished', while he is complimented on having put on weight – it makes him look 'solid' which is apparently a good thing. 'Middle-aged spread' is a natural consequence of growing older for both sexes, but women are distressed by it and many try to diet. Not only is this futile, but the stone or two that many women gain at this stage has been found to be a health benefit.

For far too long, the ageing of women has been decried by society and by women themselves, who fear the process so much that many of them will go to inordinate lengths to try to fool themselves and the rest of the world that they can escape it. The incidence of cosmetic surgery, and particularly face-lifts, is rising so fast that this kind of operation is, in certain circles, performed as routinely as dental treatment or a visit to the hairdresser. An acquaintance, who when younger, had sharp, foxy features, is, at the age of 50, more attractive than she ever was 20 years ago. Her face has filled out and softened – but, she informs me, it is 'time for a face lift'. Why? I wanted to know. Because, she said, she is 50 and things need 'tightening up'. She has been brainwashed by the culture that says that looking good is inseparable from looking young.

This is, of course, a choice open to us. We can choose to take HRT and look like Mrs Thatcher, artificially blonde at nearly 70, or like Joan Collins or Cher, both of whom have been so remade that the original woman has all but disappeared. We could, if we had the money, choose to look like Cindy Jackson, a woman whose lifelong ambition was to look like a Barbie doll and who has achieved this with numerous cosmetic operations. But do we really want to cease to be real women? How can we find our real identities if we try to deny the fact that we are growing older? Who exactly is the woman in the remade body with the face and hair that state 'I am 35' and the experience and years that make her 50? It is a contradiction, a paradox.

What right, you may say, have I to be prescriptive about these matters? None at all. It is difficult to dare to be yourself in a society which is so fundamentally looks-oriented. I can understand the feelings of a woman who dyes her grey hair before the age of 60. But if we collude with society and take as our role models those women who look 20 years younger than their chronological age, are we not denying the grace and power of older women? Should we not be claiming the right to take our place in society as we grow older without having to make ourselves something we were never meant to be? The search for identity will be confused if there is a conflict between mind and body.

Images of older women are becoming increasingly positive. Looking at the literature on the subject, I am encouraged by what is being written now – titles such as *Growing Old Disgracefully, Ourselves Growing Older: Women Ageing with Knowledge and Power, On Women Turning Fifty: Celebrating Midlife* and a book on menopause called *The Wise Woman*. But what do we mean by old? I cannot possibly agree with Germaine Greer, who says in her book *The Change* that:

Those people who deny to the fifty-year-old woman that she is old are the very people who find age shameful and obscene.

While *The Change* is an excellent and erudite book, Greer's perception of what is old is anachronistic. Her book is heavily illustrated with passages from literature, many of which were written when 50 *was* old because that was the life expectancy for women of those times. Taking as its premise the assertion that we are old at 50, her book is pessimistic. Its tone reminds me of the laconic despair of the eponymous character of T.S. Eliot's poem *The Love Song of J. Alfred Prufrock:*

> I grow old . . . I grow old . . .
> I shall wear the bottoms of my trousers rolled.

We do not have to be female Prufrocks. I look around for role models for ageing and what I find delights me. My friend Ruth, the psychotherapist, is 75, wise, serene, beautiful, at one with herself, constantly seeking to learn more, physically and mentally agile. Then there is Nancy who has just celebrated her eightieth birthday and has such a zest for life that she shames me sometimes. Nancy's secret is that *nothing* is beneath her interest. She can find the beauty and the value in everything. She reads voraciously out of a great hunger for wisdom and knowledge and her intellect is probably sharper now than when she was 50 years younger. She attends classes on a catholic range of subjects from drama to mysticism and goes to plays, concerts, meetings of all kinds.

A year ago, Nancy went into acute heart failure in the middle of the night. She rang to tell me all about it when she got out of hospital. It was so exciting, she said, because she knew that very soon she would know the answer to the greatest mystery of all. Was she not frightened? I asked her. Oh NO! she said. She couldn't wait to see what was on the other side. So great was her excitement that she rang her close friend, who was understandably shaken at hearing Nancy gasping for breath at 4.00 am in the morning – 'But I wanted to *tell* her all about it', Nancy said. Her friend called an ambulance and Nancy started what she thought was her final journey. But then, she said, she realized she could not die yet. She still had things to do and more to learn. So she decided – with a little reluctance – to postpone the lifting of the veil. She recovered quickly in hospital, baffling the doctors but not herself. She knew she had to finish what she was here for. Nancy has the greatest gift of all – a love of life combined with a total acceptance of death. She still finds the prospect exciting and is ready for it whenever it comes for her.

Margaret, aged 90, worries her 64-year-old daughter because she travels all over London, night and day on public transport. Her daughter begs her to make just one concession to her age and start taking taxis but Margaret will not hear of it. Public transport is good enough for everyone else and it's good enough for her.

With role models like this, it is difficult to define 'old' in the negative sense it is usually used. I am aware that these women are fortunate in that they have not suffered severe physical or mental deterioration, and they are not struggling to stave off hypothermia each winter – though Nancy has only her pension and a tiny, cold cottage.

One of the most inspiring books I have read on the subject of ageing is *Growing Old Disgracefully* written by a group of six women who call themselves The Hen Co-op. This book is a patchwork of stories and reflections stitched together by women who wanted to challenge the accepted views of ageing. They thought very carefully about what they wanted their book to focus on and they scrutinized the available literature. The women were conscious that they did not want their book to be about 'exceptional women: the rich and famous celebrities who were glorified for "not looking their age", another form of ageism'. Nor did they want it to be about the 'I-climbed-Mount-Everest-on-my-83rd-birthday' types. Inspiring, *yes*, but spotlighted for the very reason that they are out of the ordinary. What was missing was the voices of women like ourselves. Even the British feminist authors who have greatly enriched our understanding of women on so many levels have had very little to say about ageing women.

So they wrote about themselves and told their own stories, the stories of ordinary women growing older. They wrote this book to show that 'life can be far more exciting, more joyous and more fulfilling if you leave convention behind and start to be who *you* want to be'.

Being who we want to be is at the heart of the quest to find the woman within the mother. We have so much to celebrate and to look forward to: new directions and interests, deepening relationships with our adult children, grandchildren. And if we are fortunate, a journey through this third age which will stimulate, empower and enrich us. It is at *this* stage of our lives that we can truly 'have it all'.

Our children may leave but we never lose them. This year, my younger daughter wrote in her Mother's Day card to me: 'I hope the book is nearly finished so that you can relax for a bit and don't worry – the nest won't be empty for long. The birds may fly away but they'll return with worms in their beaks.'

The last words belong to Dorinda, who in Chapter Five (p.102) described her misery and loss of identity when her children left home. Dorinda worked through the pain to transformation:

> At last I feel like a whole person. I'm in control of my own future. All my life I have felt incompetent for anything except motherhood, held back by fear of failure. I can describe it as being like an aeroplane – I have had all the power and technology needed to fly, but I have spent all my life taxiing back and forth across the runway for fear of crashing. Now at last I have taken off and the horizons are limitless. First a woman, then a mother – all this and Heaven too.

BIBLIOGRAPHY

I recommend the following books as invaluable reading for all women at midlife, especially those facing the change of direction that inevitably occurs when children leave home.

Rowe, D. *Breaking The Bonds*, London, Fontana, 1991

Stewart, M. *Beat the Menopause without HRT*, London, Headline, 1995

Lowinsky, N.R. *The Motherline: Every Woman's Journey to Find Her Female Roots*, New York, Tarcher/Perigee, 1992

Brown, G.W. and Harris, T. *Social Origins of Depression*, London, Routledge, 1989

Posner, J. *The Feminine Mistake: Women, Work and Identity*, New York, Warner Books, 1992

Hall, J. with Jacobs, Dr R. *The Wise Woman: A Natural Approach to the Menopause*, Shaftesbury, Element Books, 1992

Hall, J. with Jacobs, Dr R. *Menopause Matters* (updated and revised edition of *The Wise Woman*), Shaftesbury, Element Books

Kaiser Stearns, A. *Coming Back: Rebuilding Lives after Crisis and Loss*, New York, Random House, 1988

Rich, A. *Of Woman Born: Motherhood as Experience and Institution*, London, Virago, 1977

Smith, S.L. *Making Peace with your Adult Children*, New York, HarperPerennial, 1993

Walker, B.G. *The Crone, Woman of Age, Wisdom and Power*, New York, HarperCollins, 1985

Secunda, V. *When You and Your Mother can't be Friends*, London, Cedar, 1993

Brown Doress, P. and Siegal, D.L. (British Edition, Shapiro, J.)

Ourselves Growing Older: Women Ageing with Knowledge and Power, London, Fontana, 1989

Ward, B. *Healing Grief: A Guide to Loss and Recovery*, London, Vermilion, 1993

Leach, P. *Children First: What Society Must Do – and is not doing – For Children Today*, London, Penguin, 1994

Knowles, J. *Love, A User's Guide*, London, Pandora, 1994

Greer, G. *The Change: Women, Ageing and the Menopause*, London, Penguin, 1992

Gibran, K. *The Prophet*, London, Heinemann, 1926, new edition, London, Pan, 1991

Hen Co-op, The, *Growing Old Disgracefully*, London, Piatkus 1993

Hen Co-op, The, *Disgracefully Yours: Inspirational Writings for Growing Older and Living Life to the Full*, London, Piatkus, 1995

Rountree, C. *On Women Turning Fifty: Celebrating Midlife Discoveries*, New York, Harper San Francisco, 1993

Shinoda Bolen, J. *Crossing to Avalon: A Woman's Midlife Pilgrimage*, New York, HarperCollins, 1994

Northrup, Dr C. *Women's Bodies, Women's Wisdom*, London, Piatkus, 1995

Tindall, G. *To the City*, London, Hutchinson, 1987

Jeffers, S. *Feel the Fear and Do It Anyway*, London and New York, Harcourt, Brace, Jovanovich, 1987

Rowe, D. *Time on our Side: Growing in Wisdom, Not Growing Old*, London, HarperCollins, 1994

MOTHERS WHO LEAVE
Behind the myth of women without their children
Rosie Jackson

In Britain an estimated 100,000 women live without their children; in the United States at least half a million. Yet mothers who've left are still thought of as unnatural, deviant, even immoral.

Drawing on her own experience and that of many other women, Rosie Jackson asks what can drive a mother to relinquish her children and examines the emotional aftermath. Exploding the myths that surround such mothers, myths ranging from vampirism to hardhearted feminism, she explores this dark side of mothering with unusual depth and sensitivity.

A close look at popular stories of mothers who leave, from *Anna Karenina* to *Kramer versus Kramer* and *Diana: Her True Story*, contrasts dramatically with the everyday reality of women's actual lives. Alongside a discussion of the most famous examples of such mothers – including Ingrid Bergman, Frieda Lawrence, Yoko Ono and Doris Lessing – Rosie Jackson unearths lesser known ones, introducing some fascinating and moving first-hand accounts.

This is a new, compassionate approach to a controversial and complex subject. Arguing that parenting as we know it must be radically rethought if women are ever to have full and equal lives, Rosie Jackson reveals the shocking personal costs of our double standards and value judgements about mothering.